# tossed

**200 fast, fresh and fabulous salads**

Published by Murdoch Books Pty Limited.

Murdoch Books Australia
Pier 8/9, 23 Hickson Road, Millers Point NSW 2000
Phone: +61 (0)2 8220 2000  Fax: +61 (0)2 8220 2558

Murdoch Books UK Limited
Erico House, 6th Floor North, 93–99 Upper Richmond Road
Putney, London SW15 2TG
Phone: + 44 (0) 20 8785 5995  Fax: + 44 (0) 20 8785 5985

Chief Executive: Juliet Rogers
Publisher: Kay Scarlett
Concept and art direction: Marylouise Brammer
Photographer: Tim Robinson
Stylist: Sarah DeNardi
Recipes by: Murdoch Books Test Kitchen
Recipe introductions by: Francesca Newby
Editors: Grace Cheetham, Katri Hilden
Designer: Annette Fitzgerald
Editorial director: Diana Hill
Production: Monika Vidovic
Stylist's assistants: Julie Ray, Loren Trompp

National Library of Australia Cataloguing-in-Publication Data
Tossed: 200 fast, fresh and fabulous salads. Includes index. ISBN 1 74045 449 9. 1. Salads. 641.83

Printed by Midas Printing (ASIA) Ltd. Printed in CHINA. First printed in 2005. Reprinted 2005, 2006  (twice).

IMPORTANT: Those who might be at risk from the effects of salmonella poisoning (the elderly, pregnant women, young children and those suffering from immune deficiency diseases) should consult their doctor with any concerns about eating raw eggs.

The publisher and stylist would like to thank the following companies for generously loaning furniture, fabric and tableware for photography: ECC Lighting and Living, Great Dane, Orrefors Kosta Boda, Georg Jensen, Royal Copenhagen, Tsunami, Villeroy & Boch, Waterford Wedgwood. Special thanks also go to the following companies: Chee Soon & Fitzgerald for their fantastic Marimekko fabrics; Design Mode International for their iittala tableware; Dinosaur Designs; Foxes for the models' clothing; Bisanna and Marble Works for tiles; Mokum Textiles for their Osborne & Little and Liberty fabrics and wallpapers; Mud; Paper Couture for their gorgeous paper lunch boxes; and Signature Prints for their Florence Broadhurst fabrics and wallpapers. Finally a heartfelt thanks to our patient models Loren, Felix, Max, Ava and Ruby and wonderful assistants Loren and Julie.

# tossed

## 200 fast, fresh and fabulous salads

Photography by Tim Robinson
Styling by Sarah DeNardi

MURDOCH BOOKS

# contents

**toss it** For far too long, salads have been relegated to the side of the plate. It's time these life-giving, energy-boosting meals were treated with a little respect. A mighty source of nutrients, a gift of nature's bounty, salads are blessed with virtues too numerous to list. For hot days, cold days, lunch with the gals or lunch on the run, nothing beats a salad, so look to your crisper and get tossing!

# toss it

There is no better **showcase** for truly fresh produce than
a salad, be it ripe tomatoes bursting with flavour, **succulent**
prawns rich with the taste of the ocean, or crumbly, creamy feta with
its salty, goaty **tang**. The joy of a great salad lies in celebrating all
the pleasures of authentic ingredients in peak condition.

The versatility of salad is one of its greatest assets. When you
need a simple meal that can be thrown together in an **instant**,
a fresh, leafy ensemble full of **crisp** raw vegetables dressed with a
classic vinaigrette is just the first option. There are infinite recipes for
absolutely gorgeous salads that involve little more effort than some
chopping and tossing, yet don't compromise on taste.

Sometimes, though, there's nothing quite so **satisfying**
as rolling up your sleeves, taking over the kitchen and creating a complex,
intricate meal offering **sophisticated** new flavours. Again,
there is a salad to suit. Experimentation is one of the great joys of
cooking, and salads offer enormous scope for innovation and discovery.
Whatever taste you are seeking out, creating a dish with a real depth

of flavour, or which somehow tastes fresh and new, is its own reward. As just one example there are wonderfully intense Asian dressings that require dozens of ingredients, four different steps and a good half hour to prepare. The deeper pleasure of taking the time to create something rare and special, especially when you're cooking for others, is an experience just begging to be shared.

There is, of course, more to salad than sheer good taste. The benefits of eating fresh vegetables are so widely acknowledged that it would be redundant to point them out again. However, we sometimes forget the value of eating a wide variety of different foods. To satisfy your body's need for the full range of vitamins and minerals, eating vegetables alone is simply not enough. We also need to find a way to include nuts, dairy, meat, seafood, fruit, seeds, pulses and grains in our diet, both in the right balance and on a regular basis. Again, here is where the humble salad comes into its own, gathering an abundance of health-giving ingredients in ways that are limited only by your taste and your imagination. A rainbow of vegetables, slivers of salty ham, shavings of Parmesan cheese, a handful of nuts and a heap of leafy greens in the one meal is more than just a good start. And eating a variety of salads throughout the week is a delicious way of ensuring you meet all your dietary needs.

Of course, salads are also a dieter's best friend. Few of us have the discipline or willpower to be sensible all of the time. The weekend blow-out is a common feature of life, whether it's the slice of cake you swore you wouldn't have, or maybe those two extra glasses of wine you definitely shouldn't have had! So if you can't be good all of the time, the next best option is to be really good most of the time. Luckily, piling up on salad during the week is an excellent way to make sure those weekend lapses don't ruin all your hard work.

Presentation is an aspect of food that is all too often just an afterthought, yet when we eat, as with all the pleasures of the body, we are engaging all our senses. Taste and smell are obviously dominant, but there is an extra element of delight involved in eating a meal that looks superb. Happily, there is something innately appealing about a mound of fresh, colourful food glistening under a light coating of dressing.

The way you choose to plate up the meal is as important as the way you dress the table. While white plates are a definite classic, there is no need to limit yourself — don't be afraid to use colour on the table, especially when serving a salad. The jewel hues of raw vegetables, the soft creamy tones of cheese and the smoky notes of roast vegetables are all enhanced by a blast of colour on the table.

Many salads look wonderful heaped high on communal platters, and there's always something invitingly intimate about serving each other at the table. Other salads are better suited to individual plates and bowls, as the construction of the meal is part of its charm. However you choose to serve the meal, give free rein to your imagination when it comes to styling the table. Quirky accessories, sensuous fabrics and arresting colours can only enhance the pleasure of eating.

The key to it all is to keep the basics simple, then dress it up with your own individual touches that reflect your personal style. Seasonal food, fresh flavours and a burst of life-affirming colour are all you really need to create a memorable meal.

**poolside** Lounging around the pool or by the barbecue on a sparkling, sunny day calls for an atmosphere of effortless luxury. When it comes to food, super-fresh, top-quality ingredients simply prepared and beautifully presented are all you need to make a splash. A sizzling barbecue and a table laden with big bowls of salad set the scene for a perfect feast in the sun.

There is no better place to soak up the long days of summer than by the pool. Big umbrellas, banana lounges and a long, cool drink are some essential props and accessories that will create the right mood, but it's the food that sits at the heart of any event. Simple, light and fresh are the key qualities of summer eating and nothing quite fits the bill like a sensational selection of salads. Nobody wants to fill right up when they're frolicking by the water. It's not just about looking good in your swimming costume but about feeling satiated, yet still light and active. Salads are the ultimate in lightweight cuisine, but you can pack a heap of super flavours into a salad without a sense of having gone over the top, or you can keep it simple by going for a leafy base topped with one or two intense additions. Either way you've got the perfect combination for a party by the pool. Stylish entertaining without the stress is the mantra of poolside dining, and salads are the perfect way to achieve that balance between easy and elegant. Keeping it casual means you can relax and join in the fun, but there's no point in entertaining if you forget to make it special. Luckily it's so simple to achieve a feeling of plenty — just lay out a spread of delectable dishes and break open a loaf of crispy, crusty bread. When dishing up poolside, take your cue from the elements and go for a simple, effortless look that reflects the myriad blues of the water and sky, smartly accented with notes of crisp white. Cool patterns and unusual accessories help bring an eclectic modern edge to a timeless setting.

15

## seared tuna, penne and green bean salad

200 g (7 oz) green beans, trimmed and cut into short lengths
300 g (10¹/2 oz) penne rigate
1 fresh tuna steak (250 g/9 oz)

125 ml (4 fl oz/¹/2 cup) olive oil
1 red onion, thinly sliced
1 tbs balsamic vinegar

Boil, steam or microwave the beans until tender but still crisp. Drain, refresh under cold water, then drain and transfer to a serving bowl.

Cook the pasta in a large pot of rapidly boiling salted water until al dente. Drain, rinse under cold water and drain again before adding to the beans.

Meanwhile, preheat a barbecue grill or chargrill pan (griddle) to medium. Brush the tuna with a little of the oil and cook for about 3–4 minutes on each side, or until seared on the outside but still pink inside. Remove from the heat, rest for 2–3 minutes and cut into thick slices.

Heat half the oil in a frying pan. Add the onion and gently sauté for about 5–6 minutes, or until softened. Add the vinegar, turn the heat up high and quickly cook until the dressing has reduced. Add the onion mixture to the pasta with the tuna and remaining oil, then lightly toss together with some salt and pepper to taste. Cool to room temperature before serving.

Serves 4

## penne with prawns

3 Roma (plum) tomatoes
375 g (13 oz) penne
500 g (1 lb 2 oz) raw prawns
    (shrimp), peeled and
    deveined, tails intact
1 tbs olive oil
100 g (3$^1$/$_2$ oz) baby English
    spinach leaves
125 g (4$^1$/$_2$ oz) goat's cheese,
    crumbled

40 g (1$^1$/$_2$ oz/$^1$/$_4$ cup) pine nuts,
    toasted

**lemon and garlic dressing**
2 garlic cloves, crushed
3 tbs extra virgin olive oil
2 tsp finely grated lemon zest
2 tbs lemon juice
1 tbs chopped flat-leaf (Italian)
    parsley

Preheat the oven to 180°C (350°F/Gas 4). Cut each tomato into six wedges and bake for 45 minutes, or until the tomatoes are just starting to dry out around the edges. Remove and cool. Meanwhile, cook the penne in a large pot of rapidly boiling salted water until al dente. Drain well, allow to cool and transfer to a large bowl.

Preheat a barbecue grill or chargrill pan (griddle) to high. Toss the prawns in the oil and cook for 2–3 minutes, or until just opaque. Mix them through the pasta with the tomato, spinach and goat's cheese. Combine the dressing ingredients and gently toss through. Sprinkle with pine nuts and serve.

Serves 4

Slippery, slithery noodles hide a host of plump, sweet prawns in this crisp and nutty, light and lively salad.

## prawn and rice noodle salad

250 g (9 oz) rice stick noodles
700 g (1 lb 9 oz) raw prawns (shrimp), peeled and deveined, tails intact
1 tbs olive oil
1 carrot, finely julienned
1 Lebanese (short) cucumber, seeded and julienned
2½ large handfuls coriander (cilantro) leaves
80 g (2¾ oz/½ cup) roasted unsalted peanuts, chopped

50 g (1¾ oz) crisp fried shallots (see Note)

dressing
125 ml (4 fl oz/½ cup) rice vinegar
1 tbs grated palm sugar
1 garlic clove, finely chopped
2 red chillies, finely chopped
3 tbs fish sauce
3 tbs lime juice
2 tbs peanut oil

Put the noodles in a large heatproof bowl, cover with boiling water and leave to soak for 10 minutes. Drain, rinse under cold water to cool, then drain again. Place in a large serving bowl.

Meanwhile, preheat a barbecue grill or chargrill pan (griddle) to high. Toss the prawns in the olive oil and cook for about 2–3 minutes, or until just opaque. Take them off the heat and toss them through the noodles with the carrot, cucumber and coriander.

To make the dressing, combine the vinegar, sugar and garlic in a small saucepan. Bring to the boil, then reduce the heat and simmer for 3 minutes to reduce slightly. Pour into a bowl and add the chilli, fish sauce and lime juice. Slowly whisk in the peanut oil, and season to taste.

Toss the dressing through the salad, scatter with the peanuts and crisp fried shallots and serve.

Note: Crisp fried shallots are red Asian shallot flakes used as a garnish in Southeast Asia. They are available from Asian food stores.

Serves 4

prawn and rice noodle salad

## chargrilled polenta with shaved fennel salad

500 ml (17 fl oz/2 cups) milk
175 g (6 oz) polenta (cornmeal)
  (don't use instant polenta)
35 g (1¼ oz/⅓ cup) grated
  Parmesan cheese, plus
  100 g (3½ oz/1 cup) shaved
  Parmesan cheese

1 tbs butter
2 baby fennel bulbs, trimmed
  (reserve the fronds)
40 g (1½ oz/1⅓ cups) picked
  watercress leaves
3 tsp lemon juice
1½ tbs olive oil

Bring the milk and 500 ml (17 fl oz/2 cups) water to the boil in a heavy-based saucepan. Add the polenta in a thin, steady stream and whisk thoroughly. Reduce the heat as low as possible and simmer for 30–40 minutes, stirring occasionally. Remove from the heat, stir in the grated Parmesan and butter and season well. Pour into an oiled square dish and leave for 30 minutes to set. When cold, cut into four squares, then cut each square diagonally to give eight triangles. Brush with a little oil and cook on a hot chargrill pan (griddle) or barbecue hotplate until crisp brown grill marks appear.

Slice the fennel very thinly and chop the fronds. Toss in a bowl with the watercress, lemon juice, oil and half the shaved Parmesan. Season well. Stack two polenta triangles on four serving plates, pile the salad on top, scatter with the remaining shaved Parmesan and serve.

Serves 4

## steamed corn salad with asian dressing

1 large red capsicum (pepper)
3 corn cobs, husks and silks
   removed
90 g (3¼ oz/1 cup) bean
   sprouts, tails trimmed
4 spring onions (scallions), thinly
   sliced on the diagonal

**asian dressing**
½ tsp crushed garlic
½ tsp finely grated fresh ginger
1 tsp sugar
1 tbs rice vinegar
1 tbs soy sauce
1 tbs lemon juice
2 tsp sesame oil
2 tbs peanut oil

Cut the capsicum into large flat pieces and remove the seeds and membranes. Cook, skin-side-up, under a hot grill (broiler) until the skin blackens and blisters. Leave to cool in a plastic bag, then peel away the skin and cut the flesh into large strips.

Slice each corn cob into six rounds. Steam for 5–8 minutes, or until tender. Arrange on a serving plate with the capsicum and bean sprouts.

Whisk all the Asian dressing ingredients together in a jug and season with pepper. Drizzle over the salad, sprinkle with the spring onion and serve.

Serves 4 as a side salad

Fresh tuna brings a tender touch to this contemporary version of a timeless French classic.

## modern salad niçoise

3 tbs lemon juice
1 garlic clove, crushed
140 ml (5 fl oz) olive oil
400 g (14 oz) waxy potatoes, such as Charlotte or kipfler
3 eggs
125 g (4½ oz) green beans, trimmed
1 green capsicum (pepper), sliced

125 g (4½ oz/heaped ¾ cup) black olives
300 g (10½ oz) firm ripe tomatoes, cut into wedges
100 g (3½ oz) cucumber, cut into chunks
3 spring onions (scallions), cut into 2 cm (¾ inch) lengths
600 g (1 lb 5 oz) fresh tuna steaks

Put the lemon juice, garlic and 125 ml (4 fl oz/½ cup) of the oil in a screw-top jar, season well and shake vigorously to combine.

Cook the potatoes in a pot of boiling salted water for 10–12 minutes, or until tender, adding the eggs for the final 8 minutes of cooking. Drain.

Cool the eggs under cold water, then peel and quarter them. Leave the potatoes to cool, then cut into chunks and place in a large bowl.

Bring another pot of lightly salted water to the boil, add the beans and blanch for 3 minutes, or until just tender. Drain and refresh under cold water. Drain well, then slice in half on the diagonal and add to the potato with the capsicum, olives, tomato, cucumber and spring onion.

Strain the garlic from the dressing, then shake again to combine. Pour half over the salad, toss through gently and transfer to a serving dish.

Meanwhile, preheat a barbecue grill or chargrill pan (griddle) to medium. Brush the tuna with the remaining oil and season well on both sides. Cook until seared on the outside and still pink inside — this will take about 3–4 minutes on each side. Remove from the heat, leave to cool for 5 minutes, then slice thinly. Arrange on top of the salad with the egg quarters, drizzle with the remaining dressing and serve.

Serves 4

chargrilled polenta
with shaved fennel salad

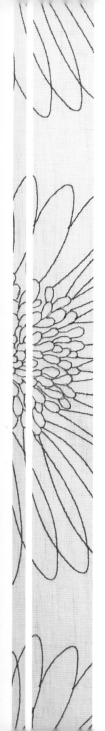

## goat's cheese, avocado and smoked salmon salad

2 tbs extra virgin olive oil
1 tbs balsamic vinegar
40 g (1¹/2 oz) baby rocket
   (arugula) leaves
1 avocado
100 g (3¹/2 oz) smoked salmon
   pieces, sliced (see Note)

8 rounds of marinated goat's
   cheese, drained
2 tbs roasted hazelnuts,
   coarsely chopped

In a large bowl, whisk together the oil and vinegar and season to taste.

Cut the avocado lengthways into quarters, then discard the skin. Place an avocado quarter on each serving plate and arrange a small pile of rocket and smoked salmon over the top.

Stack two goat's cheese rounds on each plate and scatter the hazelnuts over the top. Drizzle the dressing over, season with a good grind of black pepper and serve at once.

Note: A whole smoked trout can be used instead of the salmon. Peel away the skin, remove the bones, then flake the flesh into bite-sized pieces.

Serves 4

## marinated baby octopus salad

750 g (1 lb 10 oz) baby octopus
4 tbs olive oil
2 garlic cloves, crushed
1 red capsicum (pepper),
    thinly sliced

1 tbs sweet chilli sauce
2 tbs chopped coriander
    (cilantro)
2 tbs lime juice

Using a small, sharp knife, carefully cut between the head and tentacles of each octopus, just below the eyes. Grasp the body and push the beak out and up through the centre of the tentacles with your finger. Cut the eyes from the heads by slicing off a small disc. To clean the octopus heads, carefully slit through one side, avoiding the ink sac, and scrape out any gut from inside. Rinse well under running water and place in a large mixing bowl. Add the oil and garlic, mix well, then cover and marinate in the refrigerator for 1–2 hours.

When you're ready to eat, heat a barbecue grill or chargrill pan (griddle) to very hot. Cook the baby octopus, in batches if necessary, until just tender, about 3–5 minutes. Drain well on crumpled paper towels.

Put the capsicum, sweet chilli sauce, coriander and lime juice in a serving bowl, add the octopus and mix together. Serve warm or cold.

Serves 4

Rich, eggy mayonnaise is the only kind to use here. Slathering delicate crustaceans with a sweet gluggy slime is a crime!

## creamy seafood salad

400 g (14 oz) conchiglie (pasta shells)
250 g (9 oz/1 cup) whole-egg mayonnaise (see Note)
3 tbs fresh or 2 tbs dried tarragon
1 tbs finely chopped parsley
cayenne pepper, to taste
1 tsp lemon juice, or to taste
1 kg (2 lb 4 oz) peeled and shelled raw shellfish meat,
    such as prawns (shrimp), lobster and crab (you could
    use any one of these, or a combination)
4 tbs olive oil
2 mild red radishes, thinly sliced
1 small green capsicum (pepper), julienned

Cook the pasta in a large pot of rapidly boiling salted water until al dente. Drain, rinse under cold water and drain again. Place in a large bowl and stir through 1–2 tablespoons of the mayonnaise. Allow to cool to room temperature, stirring occasionally to prevent sticking.

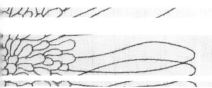

If using dried tarragon, simmer it in 3 tablespoons of milk for 3–4 minutes, then drain. Combine the tarragon, parsley, cayenne pepper and lemon juice in a bowl with the remaining mayonnaise and mix well.

Meanwhile, preheat a barbecue grill or chargrill pan (griddle) to high. Toss the shellfish meat in the oil and cook until opaque, about 2–5 minutes, depending on the thickness. Remove from the heat, cut into bite-sized pieces and add to the pasta with the radish and capsicum. Season to taste, then gently mix through the tarragon mayonnaise. Cover and chill, adding more mayonnaise or lemon juice before serving if needed.

Note: To make your own mayonnaise, whisk 2 egg yolks with 1 teaspoon of Dijon mustard and 2 teaspoons of lemon juice for 30 seconds, or until light and creamy. Add 250 ml (9 fl oz/1 cup) of light olive oil, a teaspoon at a time, whisking constantly — increase the amount of oil as the mayonnaise thickens. When all the oil has been added, stir in 2 teaspoons of lemon juice and season with salt and white pepper.

Serves 4

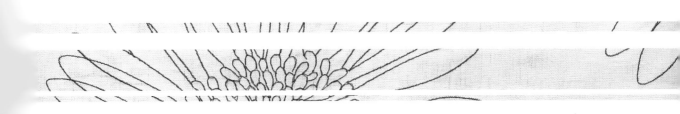

goat's cheese, avocado and
smoked salmon salad

## chargrilled cauliflower salad with sesame dressing

2 baby cos (romaine) lettuces,
    leaves separated
50 g (1³/4 oz/1²/3 cups) picked
    watercress leaves
1 head cauliflower
12 garlic cloves, crushed
2 tbs vegetable oil
2 tsp sesame seeds, toasted
1 tbs finely chopped parsley

**sesame dressing**
3 tbs tahini
1 garlic clove, crushed
3 tbs seasoned rice wine vinegar
1 tbs vegetable oil
1 tsp lime juice
¹/4 tsp sesame oil

Arrange the lettuce and watercress on a serving platter. Thoroughly whisk the sesame dressing ingredients together in a non-metallic bowl with 1 tablespoon of water until well combined. Season to taste.

Preheat a chargrill pan (griddle) or barbecue hotplate to medium. Cut the cauliflower in half, then into 1 cm (¹/2 inch) florets and spread on a baking tray. Mix together the garlic and oil, gently rub all over the cauliflower and season well. Chargrill until golden on both sides and cooked through, about 2–3 minutes. Arrange over the lettuce and watercress, drizzle with the dressing, scatter with sesame seeds and parsley and serve at once.

Serves 4 as a side salad

## spicy tomato salad with sausage

3 tomatoes, diced
1 red onion, finely chopped
1 small green capsicum
   (pepper), diced
2 tbs chopped coriander
   (cilantro)

a few drops of Tabasco sauce,
   or to taste
8 thick gourmet sausages
crusty bread, to serve

Mix together the tomato, onion, capsicum, coriander and some Tabasco sauce in a bowl. Cover and refrigerate for 1 hour, then allow to come to room temperature when you're nearly ready to serve.

Barbecue, grill (broil) or pan-fry the sausages over medium heat for about 12 minutes or until nicely browned and cooked through, turning often. Set aside to cool, then cut into thick slices.

Arrange the sausages and tomato mixture on four serving plates and serve with crusty bread.

Serves 4

Roast beef is just sublime piled on spinach and lavishly dressed with cool, creamy yoghurt laced with horseradish and lemon.

roast beef and spinach salad with horseradish cream

horseradish cream
125 g (4 1/2 oz/1/2 cup) thick plain yoghurt
1 tbs creamed horseradish
2 tbs lemon juice
2 tbs cream
2 garlic cloves, crushed
a few drops of Tabasco sauce, or to taste

200 g (7 oz) green beans, trimmed
500 g (1 lb 2 oz) rump steak
1 red onion, halved
1 tbs olive oil
100 g (3 1/2 oz) baby English spinach leaves
50 g (1 3/4 oz/1 2/3 cups) picked watercress leaves
200 g (7 oz) semi-dried (sun-blushed) tomatoes

To make the horseradish cream, whisk all the ingredients in a small bowl with a little black pepper to taste. Cover and chill for 15 minutes.

Bring a pot of lightly salted water to the boil, add the beans and blanch for 4 minutes, or until tender. Drain, refresh under cold water and drain again.

Meanwhile, preheat a griller (broiler) or barbecue hotplate to high. Brush the steak and onion halves with the oil. Cook the steak for 2 minutes on each side, or until seared but still rare, then remove from the heat, cover with foil and leave for 5 minutes. (Cook the beef a little longer if you prefer it medium or well done.) While the steak is resting, cook the onion for 2–3 minutes on each side, or until charred.

Toss the spinach, watercress, tomato and beans in a large salad bowl. Slice the beef thinly across the grain, then layer over the salad. Thinly slice the grilled onion, add to the salad and drizzle with the dressing. Season well with sea salt and freshly ground black pepper and serve.

Serves 4

roast beef and spinach salad with
horseradish cream

## egg and spinach salad with croutons

2 slices wholemeal bread,
   crusts removed
2 tsp oil
8 large English spinach leaves,
   finely shredded
150 g (5½ oz) lettuce (see Note),
   finely shredded

3 spring onions (scallions),
   finely sliced
100 g (3½ oz) button
   mushrooms, sliced
2 tbs ready-made French dressing
3 hard-boiled eggs, peeled and
   quartered

Preheat the oven to 180°C (350°F/Gas 4). Brush the bread slices with the oil. Cut them in half, then into short fingers. Spread on an oven tray and bake for 8 minutes, or until golden. Set aside to cool.

Put the spinach, lettuce, spring onion and mushrooms in a serving bowl. Drizzle with the dressing and toss lightly to combine. Add the egg quarters and croutons, gently mix together and serve at once.

Note: Any type of lettuce will suit this dish.

Serves 4 as a side salad

## pasta salad with fresh vegetables

350 g (12 oz) tri-colour spiral
   pasta
2$^1/_2$ tbs olive oil
140 g (5 oz) broccoli, cut into
   florets
5 small yellow button squash
   (about 115 g/4 oz)

1 thin carrot, sliced diagonally
175 g (6 oz/$^2/_3$ punnet) cherry
   tomatoes, halved
1$^1/_2$ tbs lemon juice
1$^1/_2$ tbs chopped parsley

Cook the pasta in a large pot of rapidly boiling salted water until al dente. Drain, rinse under cold water and drain again. Transfer to a large serving bowl and gently mix with $^1/_2$ tablespoon of the oil to prevent sticking.

Stand the broccoli and squash in a large pan of boiling water for 1 minute, then drain and plunge into iced water. Drain well, then add to the pasta with the carrot and cherry tomatoes.

Pour the lemon juice and remaining oil into a small screw-top jar and shake well. Pour over the salad, add the parsley and mix together well. Serve at room temperature.

Serves 4 as a side salad

Wonderfully soft eggplant absorbs the magical flavours of Morocco as it soaks up a wealth of warm, woody spices.

## moroccan eggplant with couscous

185 g (6½ oz/1 cup) instant couscous
200 ml (7 fl oz) olive oil
1 onion, halved and sliced
1 eggplant (aubergine)
3 tsp ground cumin
1½ tsp garlic salt
¼ tsp ground cinnamon
1 tsp paprika
¼ tsp ground cloves
50 g (1¾ oz) butter
2½ large handfuls parsley, finely chopped
zest of 1 lemon
2 tablespoons capers, rinsed and drained

Put the couscous in a large bowl and add 375 ml (1½ cups) boiling water.
Leave for 10 minutes, then fluff up with a fork.

Heat 2 tablespoons of the oil in a large frying pan and gently cook the onion for 8–10 minutes, or until nicely browned. Remove with a slotted spoon, leaving the oil in the pan.

Cut the eggplant into 1 cm ($^1/_2$ inch) thick slices, then into quarters, and place in a large bowl. Mix the cumin, garlic salt, cinnamon, paprika and cloves in a small bowl with $^1/_2$ teaspoon of salt, then sprinkle over the eggplant, tossing to coat well.

Heat the remaining oil in the frying pan over medium heat. Add the eggplant and cook, turning once, for 20–25 minutes, or until browned. Remove from the pan and allow to cool.

In the same pan, melt the butter, then add the couscous and gently cook for 2–3 minutes. Stir in the onion, eggplant, parsley, lemon zest and capers and take off the heat. Cool to room temperature before serving.

Serves 4 as a side salad

moroccan eggplant with couscous

## watercress, feta and watermelon salad

2 tbs sunflower seeds
475 g (1 lb 1 oz) rindless
  watermelon, cut into
  1 cm (3/4 inch) cubes
180 g (6 oz) feta cheese, cut
  into 1 cm (3/4 inch) cubes

75 g (2 1/2 cups) picked
  watercress sprigs
2 tbs olive oil
1 tbs lemon juice
2 tsp chopped oregano

Heat a small frying pan over high heat. Add the sunflower seeds and, shaking the pan continuously, dry-fry for 2 minutes, or until the seeds are toasted and lightly golden.

Put the watermelon, feta and watercress in a large serving dish and toss gently. Combine the oil, lemon juice and oregano in a small jug and season to taste with freshly ground black pepper (you probably won't need salt as feta is usually quite salty). Pour the dressing over the salad and toss together well. Scatter with the sunflower seeds and serve.

Serves 4 as a side salad

## cucumber salad with peanuts and chilli

3 cucumbers
2 tbs white vinegar
2 tsp white sugar
1–2 tbs sweet chilli sauce
10 French shallots (eschalots), chopped (see Note)

2 handfuls coriander (cilantro) leaves
160 g (5$^3$/$_4$ oz/1 cup) roasted unsalted peanuts, chopped
2 tbs crisp fried garlic
1 tbs fish sauce (optional)

Peel the cucumbers, cut them in half lengthways, then scoop out the seeds and slice the flesh thinly.

Combine the vinegar and sugar in a small bowl and stir until the sugar has dissolved. Transfer to a large serving bowl and add the cucumber, sweet chilli sauce to taste, shallot and coriander. Mix gently, then cover and marinate in the refrigerator for 45 minutes. Just before serving, sprinkle the salad with the peanuts, crisp fried garlic and fish sauce.

Note: If French shallots are unavailable, use 2 red onions instead.

Serves 4 as a side salad

Lemon, thyme, parsley and garlic lend a lip-smacking

pungency to soft, creamy beans and beautifully rare tuna.

### seared tuna and white bean salad

400 g (14 oz) fresh tuna steaks
1 small red onion, thinly sliced
1 tomato, seeded and chopped
1 small red capsicum (pepper), thinly sliced
2 x 400 g (14 oz) tins cannellini beans, rinsed and drained
2 garlic cloves, crushed
1 tsp chopped thyme
4 tbs finely chopped flat-leaf (Italian) parsley
oil, for brushing
100 g (3 1/2 oz) baby salad leaves or baby rocket (arugula) leaves
1 tsp lemon zest strips

### warm vinaigrette
1 1/2 tbs lemon juice
4 tbs extra virgin olive oil
1 tsp honey

Put the tuna steaks on a plate, sprinkle both sides with plenty of cracked black pepper, cover with plastic wrap and refrigerate until needed. Nearer to serving time, toss the onion, tomato and capsicum in a large mixing bowl with the beans, garlic, thyme and parsley.

To make the warm vinaigrette, put the lemon juice, oil and honey in a small saucepan, bring to the boil, then simmer, stirring, for 1 minute, or until the honey has dissolved. Remove from the heat but keep warm.

Brush a barbecue hotplate or chargrill pan (griddle) with a little oil and heat until very hot. Cook the tuna steaks for 1–2 minutes on each side, depending on their thickness — they should still be pink in the middle. Slice into large cubes and add to the beans. Pour the warm dressing over the top and toss well.

Divide the beans and tuna between four serving plates. Top with the salad leaves, scatter with the lemon zest and serve.

Serves 4

seared tuna and white bean salad

## insalata caprese

3 large vine-ripened tomatoes,
    sliced
250 g (9 oz) bocconcini cheese,
    sliced (see Note)

16–20 whole basil leaves
3 tbs extra virgin olive oil

Arrange alternating slices of tomato and bocconcini on a serving platter. Slip the basil leaves in between the tomato and bocconcini slices. Drizzle with the oil, season well with salt and ground black pepper and serve.

Note: This popular salad is most successful when made with very fresh buffalo mozzarella, if you can find it. We've used bocconcini — small balls of fresh cow's milk mozzarella — in this recipe.

Serves 4 as a side salad

## grilled tofu with broccoli and sesame dressing

200 g (7 oz) broccoli, cut
    into florets
100 g (3¹/2 oz) baby corn,
    halved lengthways
80 g (2³/4 oz) snowpeas
    (mangetout), tailed
1 large red capsicum (pepper),
    sliced

200 g (7 oz) smoked tofu,
    cut into 5 mm (¹/4 inch)
    thick slices

**sesame dressing**
3 tbs olive oil
2 tsp sesame oil
2 tbs lemon juice

Bring a pot of water to the boil and add a teaspoon of salt. Add the broccoli
and cook for 30 seconds, then add the corn and snowpeas and cook for
1 more minute. Drain, refresh under cold water, then plunge into a bowl
of cold water to cool. Drain well and toss in a serving dish with the capsicum.

Thoroughly whisk all the sesame dressing ingredients together in a small
bowl. Pour half the dressing over the salad and gently toss to combine.

Heat a barbecue grill or chargrill pan (griddle) to medium. Add the tofu
and cook for 2 minutes on each side, or until grill marks appear. Add to
the salad with the remaining dressing, toss gently and serve.

Serves 4

## red leaf salad

150 g (5¹/2 oz) mixed red lettuce
    leaves (such as coral red
    lettuce or red leaf lettuce)
1 baby fennel bulb
    (about 100 g/3¹/2 oz)
1 small red onion
2 tbs olive oil
1 tbs balsamic vinegar

Wash and dry the lettuce leaves, then tear them into bite-sized pieces.

Finely slice the fennel and onion and toss into a serving bowl with the shredded lettuce. Just before serving, drizzle the oil over the salad, then the vinegar. Toss lightly and serve.

Serves 4 as a side salad

Three types of rice lend an amazing texture to this salad, with each strain yielding a bite of its own — tender, firm and nutty.

three-rice salad

100 g (3$^1$/$_2$ oz/$^1$/$_2$ cup) long-grain white rice
110 g (3$^3$/$_4$ oz/$^1$/$_2$ cup) short-grain brown rice
95 g (3$^1$/$_4$ oz/$^1$/$_2$ cup) wild rice
1 small red capsicum (pepper)
1 small green capsicum (pepper)
3 tbs olive oil
1 garlic clove, crushed
170 g (6 oz/1$^1$/$_3$ cups) frozen baby peas, defrosted
2 tsp lemon juice
pinch of mustard powder
3 tomatoes, peeled, seeded and chopped
4 spring onions (scallions), finely chopped
3 tbs finely chopped parsley
45 g (1$^1$/$_2$ oz/$^1$/$_4$ cup) small black olives

Cook the rices separately, according to the packet instructions. Rinse, drain well, allow to cool and set aside.

Cut the capsicums into large flat pieces and remove the seeds and membranes. Cook, skin-side-up, under a hot grill (broiler) until the skins blacken and blister. Leave to cool in a plastic bag, then peel away the skin and cut the flesh into thin strips. Gently toss in a bowl with the oil and garlic, then cover and leave to marinate for at least 2 hours.

Cook the peas in a large pot of boiling salted water for 2 minutes, then refresh under cold water and drain. Put the capsicum strips in a strainer and leave to drain over a bowl to collect the oil. Whisk the oil with the lemon juice and mustard powder and season to taste with salt and pepper.

Mix together the rice, capsicum strips, peas, tomato and spring onion, then stir through the mustard dressing and parsley. Spoon onto a platter, scatter with olives and serve.

Serves 4 as a side salad

grilled tofu with broccoli and sesame dressing

## avocado and black bean salad

250 g (9 oz) dried black (turtle)
  beans
1 red onion, chopped
4 egg (Roma) tomatoes, chopped
1 red capsicum (pepper),
  chopped
375 g (13 oz) tinned corn
  kernels, drained
1 bunch coriander (cilantro),
  roughly chopped

2 avocados, chopped
1 mango, peeled and chopped
150 g (5½ oz/1 bunch) rocket
  (arugula), leaves trimmed

### lime and chilli dressing
1 garlic clove, crushed
1 small red chilli, finely chopped
2 tbs lime juice
3 tbs olive oil

Soak the beans in cold water overnight. Rinse well, drain and place in a large, heavy-based pot. Cover with cold water, bring to the boil, then reduce the heat and simmer for 1½ hours, or until tender. Drain well and allow to cool slightly.

Put the beans in a large bowl with the onion, tomato, capsicum, corn, coriander, avocado, mango and rocket. Gently toss to combine.

Whisk all the lime and chilli dressing ingredients together in a small bowl. Pour over the salad, toss gently and serve.

Serves 4

# radicchio with figs and ginger vinaigrette

1 radicchio lettuce
1 baby frisée (curly endive)
3 oranges (see Note)
1/2 small red onion, thinly
    sliced into rings
8 small green figs, quartered
3 tbs extra virgin olive oil

1 tsp red wine vinegar
1/8 tsp ground cinnamon
2 tbs orange juice
2 tbs very finely chopped glacé
    ginger, with 2 tsp syrup
2 pomegranates (optional),
    sliced in half

Wash the radicchio and frisée leaves thoroughly and drain well. Tear any large leaves into bite-sized pieces and toss in a salad bowl.

Peel and segment the oranges, discarding all the bitter white pith. Add to the salad leaves with the onion and figs, reserving eight fig quarters. Whisk the oil, vinegar, cinnamon, orange juice, ginger and ginger syrup in a small jug. Season to taste, pour over the salad and toss lightly.

Arrange the reserved figs in pairs over the salad. If you are using the pomegranates, scoop out the seeds, scatter over the salad and serve.

Note: When in season, mandarins and mandarin juice are a delicious alternative to the oranges and orange juice in this salad.

Serves 4

This superb salad can be prepared ahead, then put aside until someone summons up the energy to fire up the barbecue.

## spicy lamb and noodle salad

1 tbs five-spice powder
3 tbs vegetable oil
2 garlic cloves, crushed
2 lamb backstraps or loin fillets (about 250 g/9 oz each)
500 g (1 lb 2 oz) fresh Shanghai (wheat) noodles
1 1/2 tsp sesame oil
80 g (2 3/4 oz) snowpea (mangetout) sprouts
1/2 red capsicum (pepper), thinly sliced

4 spring onions (scallions), thinly sliced on the diagonal
2 tbs sesame seeds, toasted

ginger and chilli dressing
1 tbs finely chopped fresh ginger
1 tbs Chinese black vinegar
1 tbs Chinese rice wine
2 tbs peanut oil
2 tsp chilli oil

Combine the five-spice powder, 2 tablespoons of the vegetable oil and the garlic in a large bowl. Add the lamb and turn to coat well all over. Cover and marinate in the refrigerator for 30 minutes.

Cook the noodles in a large pot of boiling water for 4–5 minutes, or until tender. Drain, rinse with cold water and drain again. Add the sesame oil and toss to combine.

Meanwhile, preheat a barbecue grill or chargrill pan (griddle) to very hot and brush with the remaining vegetable oil. Cook the lamb for about 2–3 minutes on each side for medium-rare, or until cooked to your liking. Remove from the heat, cover with foil and leave to rest for 5 minutes, then thinly slice across the grain.

Whisk all the ginger and chilli dressing ingredients together in a small bowl until well combined.

Put the noodles, lamb strips, snowpea sprouts, capsicum and spring onion in a large bowl, pour the dressing over and toss gently to combine. Sprinkle with the sesame seeds and serve immediately.

Serves 4

radicchio with figs and ginger vinaigrette

## tofu salad

2 tsp sweet chilli sauce
1/2 tsp grated fresh ginger
1 garlic clove, crushed
2 tsp soy sauce
2 tbs sesame oil
250 g (9 oz) firm tofu

100 g (3 1/2 oz) snowpeas
  (mangetout), julienned
2 small carrots, finely julienned
100 g (3 1/2 oz/about 1 1/2 cups)
  finely shredded red cabbage
2 tbs chopped unsalted peanuts

Put the sweet chilli sauce, ginger, garlic, soy sauce and sesame oil in a small screw-top jar and shake well. Cut the tofu into 2 cm (3/4 inch) cubes and place in a bowl. Pour the marinade over, stir well, cover with plastic wrap and refrigerate for 1 hour.

Put the snowpeas in a small pan, pour over enough boiling water to cover and leave for 1 minute. Drain, plunge into iced water and drain again.

Add the snowpeas to the tofu with the carrots and cabbage and toss lightly to combine. Transfer to a serving bowl or individual plates, sprinkle with the chopped peanuts and serve.

Serves 4

## watercress salad

500 g (1 lb 2 oz/1 bunch)
   watercress, washed
1 cucumber, peeled, halved,
   seeded and thinly sliced
3 celery stalks, cut into thin
   batons
1 red onion, thinly sliced
   and separated into rings
1 bunch chives, snipped
3 oranges

60 g (2 1/4 oz/1/2 cup) chopped
   pecan nuts or walnuts

mustard citrus dressing
3 tbs olive oil
3 tbs lemon juice
2 tsp grated orange zest
1 tsp seeded mustard
1 tbs honey

Pick the watercress into small sprigs, discarding the coarser stems. Toss in a large serving bowl with the cucumber, celery, onion and chives.

Peel the oranges, removing all the bitter white pith, and cut the flesh into segments between the membrane. Add the segments to the salad.

Put all the mustard citrus dressing ingredients in a small screw-top jar, season with black pepper and shake vigorously. Pour over the salad, give a good toss, sprinkle with the nuts and serve.

Serves 4 as a side salad

An intensely fresh blast of sharp, savoury salsa swathes tender squid and crisp greens in a snappy embrace.

## squid salad with salsa verde

800 g (1 lb 12 oz) smallish squid, cleaned, scored and sliced into 4 cm (1½ inch) diamonds
2 tbs olive oil
2 tbs lime juice
150 g (5½ oz) green beans, trimmed and halved
175 g (6 oz) snowpeas (mangetout), tailed
100 g (3½ oz) baby rocket (arugula) leaves

salsa verde
1 thick slice white bread, crusts removed
140 ml (5 fl oz) olive oil
3 tbs finely chopped parsley
2 tsp finely grated lemon zest
3 tbs lemon juice
2 anchovy fillets, finely chopped
2 tbs capers, rinsed and drained
1 garlic clove, crushed

Toss the squid in a bowl with the oil, lime juice and a little salt and pepper. Cover with plastic wrap, refrigerate and leave to marinate for 2 hours.

To make the salsa verde, break the bread into chunks and drizzle with 2 tablespoons of the oil, mixing it in with your hands so it is absorbed. Place the bread and remaining oil in a food processor with the remaining salsa verde ingredients, and blend to a paste. If the mixture is too thick, thin it with a little extra lemon juice and olive oil, to taste.

Bring a pot of lightly salted water to the boil, add the beans and blanch until just tender, about 2–3 minutes. Remove with tongs, refresh under cold water, then drain well. Blanch the snowpeas in the same pot for 1 minute, then drain, refresh in cold water and drain again.

Meanwhile, preheat a barbecue grill or chargrill pan (griddle) to high. Cook the squid in batches for 3 minutes per batch, or until cooked. Take off the heat, allow to cool slightly and toss in a bowl with the beans, snowpeas and rocket. Add 3 tablespoons of salsa verde and toss gently. Arrange on a serving platter, drizzle with the remaining salsa verde and serve.

Serves 4

squid salad with salsa verde

## red cabbage salad

150 g (5¹/₂ oz/2¹/₂ cups) finely
    shredded red cabbage
125 g (4¹/₂ oz/2 cups) finely
    shredded green cabbage
2 spring onions (scallions),
    finely chopped
3 tbs olive oil

caraway dressing
2 tsp white wine vinegar
¹/₂ tsp French mustard
1 tsp caraway seeds

Put the red and green cabbage in a large serving bowl with the spring onion and mix together well.

Put all the caraway dressing ingredients in a small screw-top jar and shake well. Pour the dressing over the salad, toss lightly and serve.

Serves 4 as a side salad

## green bean and pine nut salad

280 g (10 oz) green beans,
   trimmed
1 tbs olive oil
2 tsp lemon juice
1 tbs pine nuts

4 tbs tomato juice
1 garlic clove, crushed
a few drops of Tabasco sauce,
   or to taste

Bring a pot of lightly salted water to the boil, add the beans and blanch for 2–3 minutes, or until just tender. Drain, refresh under cold water, then drain again. Toss in a bowl with the oil and lemon juice.

Put a small frying pan over high heat. Add the pine nuts and dry-fry for 3–4 minutes, or until the nuts are golden, shaking the pan frequently so they don't burn.

Put the tomato juice, garlic and some Tabasco sauce in a small pan. Bring to the boil, then reduce the heat to low and simmer, uncovered, for about 8 minutes, or until reduced by half. Allow to cool.

Arrange the beans on a serving plate, pour the tomato dressing over the top and sprinkle with the toasted pine nuts.

Serves 4 as a side salad

Sesame seeds, sesame oil and tahini open the door to a whole new world of flavour for wholesome soba noodles.

## soba noodle salad with tahini dressing

300 g (10½ oz) snake beans or green beans
300 g (10½ oz) soba noodles
4 spring onions (scallions), finely sliced
1 tbs black sesame seeds

### tahini dressing
1½ tbs tahini
2 small garlic cloves, crushed
3 tbs rice vinegar
3 tbs olive oil
1 tsp sesame oil
2 tsp soy sauce
1 tbs sugar

Trim the beans and cut into long strips on the diagonal. Bring a pot of lightly salted water to the boil, add the beans and blanch until just tender, about 2–3 minutes. Drain, refresh under cold water, then drain again.

Cook the noodles in a large pot of boiling water for 3–4 minutes, or until tender. Drain, refresh under cold water, then drain again.

Put all the tahini dressing ingredients in a screw-top jar with 1 tablespoon of warm water and shake vigorously to combine. Season to taste.

Combine the beans, noodles, spring onion and sesame seeds in a large serving bowl. When you're ready to eat, add the dressing and lightly toss together. Serve at once.

Serves 4

soba noodle salad
with tahini dressing

## cabbage with crisp fried onion

1/2 Chinese or Savoy cabbage, finely shredded

35 g (1 1/4 oz/1/2 cup) crisp fried onion (see Note)

25 g (1 oz/1/4 cup) crisp fried garlic (see Note)

1/2 red capsicum (pepper), cut into very fine strips

3 tbs mint leaves, shredded

2 red chillies, finely sliced

4 lime wedges

### dressing

4 tbs coconut milk

1 tbs fish sauce (optional)

1 tsp soft brown sugar

Arrange the cabbage on a serving platter and sprinkle with the crisp fried onion and garlic, capsicum and mint.

Combine the dressing ingredients in a small bowl and mix well. Pour over the salad, sprinkle with the chilli and serve with lime wedges.

Note: Crisp fried onion and crisp fried garlic are available in jars from Asian grocery stores. You can make your own by finely slicing peeled onion and garlic and deep-frying them in hot oil for about 30 seconds. Remove with a slotted spoon and leave to drain on crumpled paper towels. They will become crisp on sitting.

Serves 4 as a side salad

## dill potato salad

| | |
|---|---|
| 600 g (1 lb 5 oz) desiree potatoes | mayonnaise |
| 2 eggs | 1 egg yolk |
| 2 tbs finely chopped dill | 2 tsp lemon juice |
| 1½ tbs finely chopped French | 1 tsp Dijon mustard |
| shallots (eschalots) | 100 ml (3½ fl oz) light olive oil |

Bring a large pot of water to the boil. Add the potatoes and cook for 20 minutes, or until tender, adding the eggs for the last 10 minutes of cooking. Remove the potatoes and eggs from the pan and allow to cool.

Peel the potatoes, then cut into 2–3 cm (³/4–1¹/4 inch) cubes and place in a large bowl. Peel and chop the eggs and add to the potatoes with the dill and shallot. Gently toss to combine, then season.

To make the mayonnaise, put the egg yolk, lemon juice, mustard and a pinch of salt in a food processor. With the motor running, gradually add the oil a few drops at a time. When about half the oil has been added, add the remaining oil in a thin, steady stream until it has all been incorporated. Gently stir the mayonnaise through the potato salad using a large metal spoon and serve.

Serves 4 as a side salad

## moroccan lamb salad

spice mix
2 garlic cloves, crushed
1 tsp ground cumin
1 tsp harissa (see Note)
1 tsp ground coriander

125 ml (4 fl oz/$^1$/$_2$ cup) olive oil
2 large handfuls coriander,
    finely chopped
2 tbs lemon juice
3 tbs chopped parsley
$^1$/$_2$ tsp ground turmeric
2 lamb backstraps or loin fillets
    (600 g/1 lb 5 oz), trimmed
250 g (9 oz/1 cup) thick plain
    yoghurt

50 g (1$^3$/$_4$ oz) baby rocket
    (arugula) leaves

pistachio couscous
125 ml (4 fl oz/$^1$/$_2$ cup)
    orange juice
2 tbs lemon juice
$^1$/$_2$ tsp ground cinnamon
250 g (9 oz/1$^1$/$_3$ cups) instant
    couscous
50 g (1$^3$/$_4$ oz) butter
35 g (1$^1$/$_4$ oz/$^1$/$_4$ cup) currants
50 g (1$^3$/$_4$ oz/heaped $^1$/$_3$ cup)
    chopped pistachio nuts
425 g (15 oz) tin chickpeas,
    rinsed and drained
3 tbs chopped parsley

In a small bowl, combine the spice mix ingredients. Put the oil in a large,
non-metallic bowl and stir in half the spice mix and all the coriander,
lemon juice, parsley and turmeric. Mix well. Add the lamb, turning to coat
well. Cover with plastic wrap and refrigerate for 1 hour.

Mix the remaining spice mix together with the yoghurt, then cover and refrigerate until needed.

To make the pistachio couscous, pour the orange juice and lemon juice into a measuring jug, then add enough water to make 300 ml (10$^{1}/_{2}$ fl oz). Pour into a saucepan, add the cinnamon and bring to the boil. Remove from the heat, pour in the couscous, cover and leave for 5 minutes. Add the butter and fluff up the couscous with a fork, raking out any lumps, then fold in the currants, pistachios, chickpeas and parsley.

Meanwhile, preheat a barbecue grill or chargrill pan (griddle) to high. Drain the marinade from the lamb and cook for 2 minutes on each side, or until charred on the outside but still pink in the middle. Remove from the heat, cover with foil and rest for 5 minutes, then slice across the grain.

Divide the couscous between four large serving plates and top with the rocket and lamb slices. Top with a dollop of the yoghurt mixture and serve.

Note: Harissa is a fiery Middle Eastern chilli paste readily available from delicatessens or specialist food stores.

Serves 4

moroccan lamb salad

## three-bean salad

100 g (3¹/2 oz) green beans,
    trimmed and cut into
    4 cm (1¹/2 inch) lengths
200 g (7 oz) frozen broad (fava)
    beans, defrosted
310 g (10¹/2 oz) tin butter
    beans, rinsed and drained

310 g (10¹/2 oz) tin red kidney
    beans, rinsed and drained
1 small red onion, finely sliced
2 tbs chopped parsley
2 tbs ready-made French
    dressing

Bring a small pot of lightly salted water to the boil. Add the green beans and broad beans. Stand for 1 minute over the heat, then drain. Refresh under cold water, then drain again.

Place the green beans and broad beans in a serving bowl with all the tinned beans, onion and parsley. Pour the dressing over and toss well.

Serves 4 as a side salad

## roasted tomato and pasta salad with pesto

140 ml (5 fl oz) olive oil
500 g (1 lb 2 oz/2 punnets)
    cherry tomatoes
5 garlic cloves, unpeeled
400 g (14 oz) orecchiette or
    other shell-shaped pasta

90 g (3¼ oz/⅓ cup)
    ready-made pesto
3 tbs balsamic vinegar
basil leaves, to serve

Preheat the oven to 180°C (350°F/Gas 4). Put 2 tablespoons of the oil in a roasting tin and leave to warm in the hot oven for 5 minutes. Add the cherry tomatoes and garlic, season well and toss until the tomatoes are well coated. Return to the oven and roast for 20 minutes (be sure to keep all the pan juices for the dressing).

Meanwhile, cook the pasta in a large pot of rapidly boiling salted water until al dente. Drain well and transfer to a large serving bowl.

Squeeze the flesh from the roasted garlic cloves into a bowl. Add the remaining oil, pesto, vinegar and 3 tablespoons of the pan juices from the roasted tomatoes. Season with a little salt and pepper, then toss to combine. Add to the pasta and mix well to coat. Gently stir in the roasted tomatoes, then scatter with basil leaves. Serve warm or cold.

Serves 4

Succulent slices of juicy rare beef strike up a tender harmony with silky-smooth strips of eggplant.

## chargrilled beef and eggplant salad

2 eggplants (aubergines)
2 tbs salt
3 zucchini (courgettes), cut into 2 cm (3/4 inch) chunks
2 red capsicums (peppers), sliced into 2 cm (3/4 inch) strips
100 g (31/2 oz) button mushrooms, halved
2 onions, thickly sliced
3 tbs olive oil
1 tbs lemon juice
oil, for brushing
750 g (1 lb 10 oz) sirloin or rump steak, trimmed
40 g (11/2 oz) snowpea (mangetout) sprouts
1 small handful shredded basil

Chop the eggplants in half lengthways, then lay them cut-side-down and cut them into long slices about 1 cm (1/2 inch) thick. Spread the slices in a single layer on a plate and sprinkle with the salt. Set aside for 15 minutes, then rinse and pat dry thoroughly.

Meanwhile, toss the zucchini, capsicum, mushroom and onion in a large bowl with the oil and lemon juice. Cover with plastic wrap and leave for 30 minutes at room temperature.

Preheat a barbecue hotplate or chargrill pan (griddle) to high. Lightly brush with oil, add the beef and cook for 2 minutes on each side to seal, turning once. Move the meat to a cooler part of the barbecue and cook for a further 2 minutes on each side for a medium-rare result. Transfer to a plate and cover loosely with foil. Leave to cool, then slice thinly.

While the beef is resting, remove the vegetables from the marinade. Cook the vegetables and eggplant strips in batches on the barbecue for about 5 minutes each, or until just tender and browned.

Arrange a pile of snowpea sprouts on four serving plates. Top with the beef slices and vegetables, scatter with basil and serve at once.

Serves 4

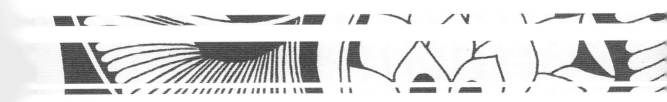

roasted tomato and pasta
salad with pesto

## spaghetti, olive and tomato salad

350 g (12 oz) spaghetti or
   bucatini pasta
2¹/₂ large handfuls basil
   leaves, shredded
250 g (9 oz/1 punnet) cherry
   tomatoes, halved
1 garlic clove, crushed

50 g (1³/₄ oz/¹/₃ cup) chopped
   black olives
3 tbs olive oil
1 tbs balsamic vinegar
35 g (1¹/₄ oz/¹/₃ cup) grated
   Parmesan cheese

Cook the pasta in a large pot of rapidly boiling salted water until al dente. Drain, rinse under cold water and drain again.

Toss the basil, cherry tomatoes, garlic, olives, oil and vinegar in a serving bowl. Set aside for about 15 minutes to allow the flavours to develop, then mix in the drained pasta. Add the Parmesan, and salt and pepper to taste. Toss well and serve immediately.

Serves 4

## easy barbecued chicken and pasta salad

1 small barbecued chicken
350 g (12 oz) penne pasta
3 tbs olive oil
2 tbs white wine vinegar
250 g (9 oz/1 punnet) cherry
    tomatoes, halved

1 large handful basil leaves,
    chopped
50 g (1 3/4 oz/1/3 cup) chopped
    black olives

Pull the meat and skin from the barbecued chicken and finely shred it.

Cook the pasta in a large pot of rapidly boiling salted water until al dente. Drain well, then transfer to a serving bowl. Combine the oil and vinegar and toss through the pasta while it is still warm.

Add the shredded chicken, cherry tomatoes, basil and olives and toss to combine. Sprinkle with freshly ground black pepper and serve warm.

Serves 4

The humble chicken hits fresh new heights when given a smart dressing down by a piquant salsa verde.

## chicken with green chilli salsa verde

**green chilli salsa verde**
1 green capsicum (pepper), roughly chopped
1–2 long green chillies, seeded and chopped
1 garlic clove, chopped
1 handful flat-leaf (Italian) parsley
1 handful basil
3 spring onions (scallions), finely chopped
1 tbs lemon juice
1 tbs olive oil

4 chicken breast fillets (about 200 g/7 oz each)
70 g (2 1/2 oz/2 1/3 cups) watercress sprigs
3 celery stalks, sliced

To make the salsa verde, put the capsicum, chilli, garlic, parsley and basil in a food processor and blend to a purée. Transfer the mixture to a sieve and leave to sit for 20 minutes to drain, then transfer to a bowl and stir in the spring onion, lemon juice and oil. Season with salt and pepper.

Meanwhile, preheat a barbecue grill or chargrill pan (griddle) to medium. Add the chicken and cook for 6–8 minutes on one side. Turn and cook for a further 5 minutes, or until cooked through — the exact cooking time will vary depending on the heat of your barbecue and the thickness of your chicken fillets. Leave to cool slightly, then shred into a large bowl.

While the chicken is still warm, add the salsa verde and toss to coat well. Combine the watercress and celery in a serving dish, top with the chicken and salsa verde mixture, toss gently and serve at once.

Serves 4

chicken with green chilli salsa verde

## coleslaw with lime mayonnaise

175 g (6 oz/2$^1$/$_2$ cups) shredded red cabbage

175 g (6 oz/2$^1$/$_2$ cups) shredded white cabbage

115 g (4 oz/$^3$/$_4$ cup) grated carrot

120 g (4 oz/1$^1$/$_3$ cups) bean sprouts, tails trimmed

2 large handfuls coriander leaves, finely chopped

3 spring onions (scallions), finely sliced

### lime mayonnaise

2 egg yolks

1 tbs soy sauce

1 bird's eye chilli, finely chopped

3 tbs lime juice

200 ml (7 fl oz) olive oil

Toss the red and green cabbage, carrot, bean sprouts, coriander and spring onion together in a large bowl.

To make the lime mayonnaise, put the egg yolks, soy sauce, chilli, lime juice and a pinch of salt in a food processor. With the motor running, gradually add the oil a few drops at a time. When about half the oil has been added, add the remaining oil in a thin, steady stream until it has all been incorporated. Add 1 tablespoon of warm water and blend well.

Mix enough lime mayonnaise through the coleslaw to coat (any leftover mayonnaise can be refrigerated for 1 week). Refrigerate until ready to serve.

Serves 4 as a side salad

## classic coleslaw

1/2 small green cabbage
1/4 small red cabbage
2 carrots, coarsely grated
4 radishes, coarsely grated
1/2 red capsicum (pepper),
   chopped

3 spring onions (scallions), sliced
3 tbs chopped parsley
175 g (6 oz/2/3 cup) ready-made
   whole-egg mayonnaise

Remove the hard core from the cabbages and shred the leaves with a sharp knife. Toss in a large bowl and add the carrot, radish, capsicum, spring onion and parsley. Refrigerate until ready to serve.

Just before serving, add the mayonnaise, season to taste with salt and freshly ground black pepper and toss until well combined.

Serves 4 as a side salad

Sweet, juicy mango is the perfect partner to soft, flaky salmon and together they're pretty as a picture — a symphony in pink.

## seared asian salmon salad

700 g (1 lb 9 oz) salmon fillets
1 tbs olive oil
2 tbs lime juice
1 tbs soy sauce
2 tbs runny honey
2 ripe mangoes, peeled and
    thinly sliced
200 g (7 oz) bean sprouts,
    tails trimmed
1 small cos (romaine) lettuce,
    leaves separated

1 handful coriander (cilantro)
    leaves

### asian dressing
1 tbs olive oil
1 tbs fish sauce
2 tbs lime juice
1 small red chilli, finely chopped
1/2 tsp sugar

Remove any pin bones from the salmon and put the fillets in a single layer in a shallow non-metallic dish. In a small bowl, whisk the oil, lime juice, soy sauce and honey. Pour the mixture over the salmon, ensuring it coats all sides of the fish. Cover and refrigerate for 30 minutes.

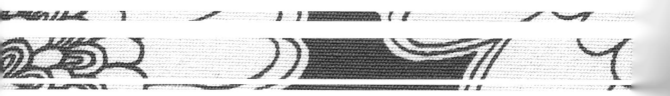

Meanwhile, put all the Asian dressing ingredients in a small bowl and whisk until well combined. Set aside until needed.

Preheat a barbecue grill or chargrill pan (griddle) to high. If you like your salmon slightly pink in the middle, cook the fillets for 5 minutes on one side, then turn and cook the second side for a further 4 minutes. If you prefer it cooked all the way through, leave it for an extra minute on the second side. The exact cooking time will vary depending on the heat of your barbecue and the thickness of your salmon fillets. Leave the salmon to cool slightly, then break into chunks.

Put the mango, bean sprouts and lettuce leaves in a serving bowl, add the salmon chunks and toss gently. Pour over the dressing, scatter with the coriander and serve at once.

Note: Add the dressing just before serving so the bean sprouts and lettuce leaves don't become soggy.

Serves 4

seared asian salmon salad

## greek salad

4 tomatoes, cut into wedges
1 telegraph (long) cucumber,
    peeled, halved, seeded and
    diced into small cubes
2 green capsicums (peppers),
    cut into strips
1 red onion, finely sliced
16 Kalamata olives

250 g (9 oz) firm feta cheese,
    cut into cubes
3 tbs flat-leaf (Italian) parsley
12 mint leaves
125 ml (4 fl oz/1/2 cup) olive oil
2 tbs lemon juice
1 garlic clove, crushed

Put the tomato, cucumber, capsicum, onion, olives, feta and half the parsley and mint leaves in a large serving bowl. Toss together gently.

Combine the oil, lemon juice and garlic in a small screw-top jar, season well and shake until thoroughly combined. Pour the dressing over the salad, toss well and serve scattered with the remaining parsley and mint.

Serves 4 as a side salad

## wild and brown rice salad

65 g (2¼ oz/⅓ cup) wild rice
135 g (5 oz/⅔ cup) long-grain
    brown rice
1 small red onion, finely diced
½ red capsicum (pepper),
    finely chopped
1 celery stalk, thinly sliced
1½ tbs chopped parsley
30 g (1 oz/¼ cup) chopped
    pecan nuts

citrus dressing
2 tbs orange juice
2 tbs lemon juice
1 teaspoon finely grated
    orange zest
½ tsp finely grated lemon
    zest
3 tbs olive oil

Cook the wild rice in a pot of boiling water for 30–40 minutes, or until just tender. Drain well, then allow to cool. Meanwhile, boil the brown rice for 25–30 minutes or until just tender, then drain well and allow to cool. Toss all the rice in a bowl with the onion, capsicum, celery and parsley.

Put a frying pan over medium heat. Add the pecans and dry-fry, stirring often, for 2–3 minutes, or until lightly toasted. Spread on a plate to cool.

Whisk all the citrus dressing ingredients together in a small bowl, pour over the salad and gently fold through. Mix in the pecans just before serving.

Serves 4 as a side salad

Black vinegar adds a dark complexity to the dressing, bringing a savoury depth to this crunchy salad.

asian chicken salad with black vinegar dressing

600 g (1 lb 5 oz) chicken breast fillets
1 large carrot, julienned
100 g (3 1/2 oz) baby Asian greens
1 Lebanese (short) cucumber, julienned
200 g (7 oz/2 heaped cups) bean sprouts, tails trimmed
3 spring onions (scallions), sliced on the diagonal
1 small handful Thai basil leaves

black vinegar dressing
2 tbs black vinegar
2 tbs kecap manis
1 1/2 tbs soy sauce
1 tsp sesame oil
2 tbs vegetable oil
5 cm (2 inch) piece of fresh ginger, peeled and grated

Heat a barbecue hotplate or chargrill pan (griddle) to medium. Add the chicken and cook for 6–8 minutes on one side. Turn and cook for a further 5 minutes, or until just cooked through — the exact cooking time will vary depending on the heat of your barbecue and the thickness of the chicken fillets. Remove from the heat and leave to cool slightly.

Meanwhile, make the black vinegar dressing. Pour the vinegar, kecap manis and soy sauce into a bowl and whisk together. Add the sesame oil and vegetable oil, whisk well, then stir in the ginger and set aside.

Shred or slice the chicken and toss in a serving bowl with the carrot, baby Asian greens and cucumber. Pour over the dressing and toss gently. Scatter with the bean sprouts, spring onion and basil and serve.

Serves 4

asian chicken salad with black vinegar dressing

## spicy potato and bean salad

350 g (12 oz) baby new
    potatoes, halved
165 g (5¾ oz) green beans,
    trimmed and halved
    diagonally

coriander dressing
3–4 tbs olive oil
1 red chilli, seeded and sliced
1 garlic clove, crushed
3 tbs chopped coriander
    (cilantro)
3 tsp red wine vinegar
1/2 teaspoon caraway seeds

Put the potatoes in a large pot of gently simmering water and cook for 20 minutes, or until tender but still firm. Drain and set aside.

Bring a pot of lightly salted water to the boil, add the beans and blanch for 2–3 minutes, or until bright green and just tender. Drain, refresh under cold water, then drain again. Put in a serving bowl with the potatoes.

To make the coriander dressing, whisk all ingredients together in a small bowl until well combined. Pour the dressing over the potatoes, toss well and serve at once, so the salad doesn't discolour.

Serves 4 as a side salad

## waldorf salad

lettuce leaves, to serve
2 red apples, quartered and
    cored
1 large green apple, quartered
    and cored

1½ celery stalks, sliced
25 g (1 oz/½ cup) walnut halves
2 tbs ready-made mayonnaise
1 tbs sour cream

Line a serving bowl with lettuce leaves. Cut the apples into 2 cm (¾ inch) chunks and place in a large mixing bowl with the celery and walnuts.

In a small bowl, combine the mayonnaise and sour cream and mix well. Fold the dressing through the apple, celery and walnut mixture, then transfer to the lettuce-lined serving bowl and serve at once.

Serves 4 as a side salad

Substantial yet summery, this one-pot wonder won't burst the seams of your itsy-bitsy, teeny-weeny, yellow polka-dot bikini.

## potato and prawn salad

800 g (1 lb 12 oz) waxy potatoes (such as chats, pink fir apple or kipfler), scrubbed
650 g (1 lb 7 oz) large raw prawns (shrimp), peeled and deveined, tails intact
200 g (7 oz/2 small bunches) rocket (arugula), leaves trimmed and torn, or 150 g (5 1/2 oz) baby rocket (arugula) leaves
2 avocados, diced

### red wine vinegar dressing
125 ml (4 fl oz/1/2 cup) olive oil
3 tbs red wine vinegar
2 tsp mustard powder
2 tbs finely chopped dill

Put the potatoes in a large pot of salted water and bring to the boil. Reduce the heat and simmer rapidly for 12–15 minutes, or until tender when pierced with a sharp knife. Drain well, allow to cool a little, then slice any large potatoes, keeping the small ones whole. Transfer to a serving dish.

Whisk all the red wine vinegar dressing ingredients together in a small bowl until thoroughly combined. Season with salt and black pepper and pour two-thirds of the dressing over the potatoes. Toss gently and set aside.

Meanwhile, preheat a barbecue grill or chargrill pan (griddle) to high. Cook the prawns for 2 minutes on one side, or until just starting to turn pink. Turn them over and cook for 1 minute more, or until just cooked through. Add them to the potatoes along with the rocket and avocado. Pour over the remaining dressing, toss gently and serve at once.

Note: This salad can also be served cold. If you're making it in advance, dress the potatoes with two-thirds of the dressing, but mix through the avocado, rocket and remaining dressing just before serving.

Serves 4

potato and prawn salad

## fast melon salad

1 honeydew melon
45 g (1 1/2 oz/1 1/2 cups)
  watercress sprigs
1 large avocado, sliced
1 red capsicum (pepper),
  thinly sliced
150 g (5 1/2 oz) marinated feta
  cheese, cubed

60 g (2 oz/1/3 cup) marinated
  Niçoise olives

**dressing**
2 tbs olive oil
1 1/2 tbs white wine vinegar
1 teaspoon Dijon mustard

Cut the melon into slices and discard the rind. Arrange the melon slices on a large platter. Scatter with the watercress sprigs, then arrange the avocado, capsicum, feta and olives over the top.

Put all the dressing ingredients in a small screw-top jar. Shake until well combined and drizzle over the salad.

Serves 4 as a side salad

## green papaya salad

500 g (1 lb 2 oz) green papaya, peeled and seeded (see Note)

2 small red chillies, thinly sliced

1 tbs grated palm sugar or soft brown sugar

1 tbs soy sauce

2 tbs lime juice

1 tbs crisp fried garlic (see Note)

1 tbs crisp fried shallots (see Note)

50 g (1³/₄ oz) green beans, trimmed and cut into 1 cm (¹/₂ inch) lengths

8 cherry tomatoes, quartered

2 tbs chopped roasted unsalted peanuts

Grate the papaya into long, fine shreds with a grater or a knife. Place in a large mortar and pestle with the chilli, sugar, soy sauce and lime juice and lightly pound until combined. Add the crisp fried garlic and shallots, beans and cherry tomatoes. Lightly pound for another minute or two, or until combined. Serve immediately, sprinkled with the peanuts.

Note: Green papaya and packets of crisp fried garlic and shallots are available from Asian grocery stores.

Serves 4 as a side salad

Soft and fluffy on the inside, these scrumptious baked potatoes are loaded with tasty salad. Even the kids will love them.

## baked potatoes filled with salad

4 large baking potatoes
   (about 365 g/12$^1$/$_2$ oz each)
4 slices prosciutto
310 g (10$^1$/$_2$ oz) tin corn
   kernels, drained
2 celery stalks, sliced
100 g (3$^1$/$_2$ oz) baby English
   spinach leaves

dressing
2$^1$/$_2$ tbs tomato juice
1$^1$/$_2$ tbs red wine vinegar
2 tbs olive oil

Preheat the oven to 200°C (400°F/Gas 6). Thoroughly scrub the skins of the potatoes and prick them several times. Transfer to a roasting tin and bake, uncovered, for 1 hour, or until tender when pierced with a sharp knife. (If you're in a hurry, you could microwave the potatoes on high, uncovered, for about 20 minutes, putting one potato in the centre of the microwave and spreading the others out around it.)

Meanwhile, whisk all the dressing ingredients together in a small bowl. Season with salt and pepper and set aside.

Put a frying pan over high heat. Add the prosciutto and dry-fry for a few minutes on both sides, or until nice and crispy. Break the prosciutto into small pieces and set aside.

Sit the potatoes on a chopping board and make two deep incisions crossways over the top so they open out into quarters — be careful not to cut all the way through; the potatoes should still be attached at the base.

Put the corn, celery and spinach in a large bowl, pour over two-thirds of the dressing and toss well. Sit the potatoes on four serving plates and spoon a little dressing into each potato. Spoon the salad mixture into each potato, letting it spill over a little. Top with prosciutto and serve at once.

Serves 4

baked potatoes filled with salad

## green pawpaw salad

**tamarind dressing**
2 tbs fish sauce
1 1/2 tbs tamarind purée
3 tsp lime juice
2 tbs grated palm sugar

1 green pawpaw, peeled,
   seeded and grated

60 g (2 1/4 oz) snake beans, sliced
1 garlic clove
1 small red chilli, chopped
3 tsp dried shrimp
6 cherry tomatoes, halved
1 handful coriander (cilantro)
   sprigs
2 tbs chopped roasted peanuts

To make the tamarind dressing, put all the ingredients in a small bowl. Mix well to dissolve the sugar and set aside. Put the grated pawpaw in a bowl, sprinkle with salt and allow to stand for 30 minutes. Rinse well.

Blanch the beans in a pot of lightly salted boiling water until just tender, about 2–3 minutes. Drain and refresh under cold water, then drain again.

Pound the garlic and chilli to a fine paste in a large mortar and pestle. Add the dried shrimp and pound until puréed. Add the pawpaw and beans and lightly pound for 1 minute. Add the tomato and pound briefly to bruise, then mix in the coriander. Spoon onto four serving plates and pour the dressing over the top. Sprinkle with the peanuts and serve.

Serves 4 as a side salad

## green and yellow bean salad

175 g (6 oz) green beans,
    trimmed
175 g (6 oz) yellow beans,
    trimmed
2 tbs olive oil

3 tsp lemon juice
1 garlic clove, crushed
shaved Parmesan cheese,
    to serve

Bring a pot of lightly salted water to the boil. Add the green and yellow beans and blanch until just tender, about 2–3 minutes. Drain, refresh under cold water, then drain again.

Put the oil, lemon juice and garlic in a bowl, season with salt and freshly ground black pepper and mix well. Arrange the beans in a serving bowl, pour the dressing over and toss to coat. Scatter with Parmesan and serve.

Serves 4 as a side salad

Olives and capers fire intense bursts of flavour into seductively salty haloumi, hosed down by cooling cubes of cucumber.

## grilled haloumi salad with herb dressing

1 large Lebanese (short) cucumber, seeded and diced
3 tomatoes, seeded and diced
40 g (1 1/2 oz/1/4 cup) pitted and halved Kalamata olives
2 tbs capers, rinsed and drained
1 small red onion, finely diced
300 g (10 1/2 oz) haloumi cheese, cut into 1 cm (1/2 inch) slices

### herb dressing
1 garlic clove, roughly chopped
1 small handful basil leaves
1 small handful flat-leaf (Italian) parsley
3 tbs olive oil
2 tbs lemon juice

Heat a barbecue grill or chargrill pan (griddle) to medium. While it is heating, prepare the salad: simply put the cucumber, tomato, olives, capers and onion in a serving dish and mix together gently.

To make the herb dressing, crush the garlic in a mortar and pestle with a pinch of salt. Add the basil and parsley and pound until a paste starts to form. Add a little of the oil and pound for another 10 seconds. Stir in the remaining oil and lemon juice and season with black pepper. (If you prefer, purée the ingredients in a food processor.) Set aside.

Chargrill the haloumi for about 1–2 minutes on each side, or until it is starting to soften but not melt. Cut the haloumi into thick strips and arrange on top of the salad. Spoon the dressing over the top and serve at once while the haloumi is still hot, before it becomes rubbery and tough.

Serves 4

grilled haloumi salad with
herb dressing

**ladies who lunch**   Lingering over an elegant lunch with the
ladies who matter the most to you can be a wicked and gossipy
delight. Keep it fresh and keep it light, as a virtuous lunch leaves

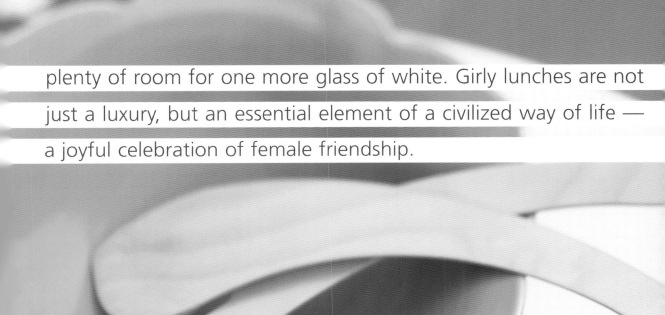

plenty of room for one more glass of white. Girly lunches are not just a luxury, but an essential element of a civilized way of life — a joyful celebration of female friendship.

Banish any notion of ladies who lunch as idle creatures with too much time and money and not enough to do. Lunching with your girlfriends is one of life's most sublime pleasures and a luxury available to all of us — an exploration of lives, loves and longings. Even if your mates are a gaggle of goodtime girls, the chances are most of you will be watching your waistline. If there's a time to count kilojoules, carbohydrates and fat of all kinds this is it, so keep this chapter close at hand. All the recipes assembled within it are either low carb or low fat, specifically suited to the diet-conscious eater. You can enjoy these luscious salads to your heart's content, without sacrificing good taste on the altar of shapeliness. Plating it up is another delicious aspect of putting on a girly lunch — if you've ever yearned to indulge your inner child, the one who secretly longs for something pretty in pink, this is the time to cut loose. Florals, pinks and pretty napkins don't have to be fusty and faded, nor should delicate china be relegated to the back of the cupboard. Pull it all out and funk it up with a shot of intense colour or search around for a pearly pink made fresh with a modish pattern. Whether you lean towards Jane Austen or Marilyn Monroe there are myriad ways to make it pretty but keep it modern. Sacrifice is not a notion that should play a part in any celebration, even an everyday one. Moderation can be the enemy of variety and flavour, but you can make it moreish without being bad. Serve up salads and your girlfriends will thank you when they indulge in that extra glass.

## scallop, ginger and spinach salad

300 g (10½ oz) scallops,
    without roe
oil, for brushing
100 g (3½ oz) baby English
    spinach leaves
1 small red capsicum (pepper),
    very finely julienned
50 g (1¾ oz/heaped ½ cup)
    bean sprouts, tails trimmed

**sake dressing**
25 ml (1 fl oz) sake
1 tbs lime juice
2 tsp shaved palm sugar or
    soft brown sugar
1 tsp fish sauce

Slice or pull off any vein, membrane or hard white muscle from the scallops. Rinse the scallops and pat dry with paper towels. Put all the sake dressing ingredients in a small bowl and mix until the sugar has dissolved.

Heat a chargrill pan (griddle) or barbecue hotplate to high and lightly brush with oil. Cook the scallops in batches for 1 minute on each side, or until just cooked.

Divide the spinach, capsicum and bean sprouts between four plates. Arrange the scallops on top, pour over the dressing and serve at once.

Serves 4

## vietnamese prawn salad

1/2 Chinese cabbage
1/2 red onion, finely sliced
500 g (1 lb 2 oz) cooked tiger
    prawns (shrimp), peeled
    and deveined, tails intact
1 handful coriander (cilantro)
    leaves, chopped
1 handful Vietnamese mint
    leaves, chopped

whole Vietnamese mint leaves,
    to serve

dressing
2 tbs sugar
2 tbs fish sauce
3 tbs lime juice
1 tbs white vinegar

Shred the cabbage finely and place in a large bowl. Cover with plastic wrap and chill for 30 minutes.

Just before serving, put all the dressing ingredients in a small jug with 1/2 teaspoon salt and mix well to dissolve the sugar.

In a serving bowl, toss together the shredded cabbage, onion, prawns, coriander and mint. Pour over the dressing, toss through gently, garnish with a few whole mint leaves and serve.

Serves 4

Chargrilling tofu leaves it slightly chewy on the edges yet soft as silk inside, perfect for soaking up the earthy miso.

## marinated tofu salad with ginger miso dressing

marinade
4 tbs tamari, shoyu or light
    soy sauce
2 tsp peanut or vegetable oil
2 garlic cloves, crushed
1 tsp grated fresh ginger
1 tsp chilli paste
1/2 teaspoon salt

ginger miso dressing
2 tsp white miso paste
2 tbs mirin
1 tsp sesame oil

1 tsp grated fresh ginger
1 tsp finely snipped chives
1 tbs toasted sesame seeds

500 g (1 lb 2 oz) firm tofu, diced
    into 2 cm (3/4 inch) cubes
2 tsp oil
400 g (14 oz) mixed salad leaves
1 Lebanese (short) cucumber,
    finely sliced
250 g (9 oz/1 punnet) cherry
    tomatoes, halved

In a bowl, mix together all the marinade ingredients. Add the tofu and gently mix until well coated. Marinate for at least 10 minutes, or preferably for a few hours or overnight. When you're ready to cook, drain the tofu, reserving the marinade.

To make the ginger miso dressing, combine the miso paste with 125 ml (4 fl oz/$1/2$ cup) of hot water and leave until the miso dissolves. Add the mirin, sesame oil, ginger, chives and sesame seeds and stir well until the mixture begins to thicken. Set aside.

Preheat a chargrill pan (griddle) or barbecue hotplate to medium. Brush with the oil, add the tofu and cook, turning now and then, for about 4 minutes, or until golden brown all over. Pour on the reserved marinade and cook the tofu for another minute over high heat. Remove from the heat and allow to cool for 5 minutes.

Meanwhile, toss the salad leaves, cucumber and tomato in a serving bowl. Add the tofu, drizzle with the dressing, toss well and serve.

Serves 4

scallop, ginger and spinach salad

## roast duck salad with chilli dressing

**chilli dressing**
1/2 tsp chilli flakes
2 1/2 tbs fish sauce
1 tbs lime juice
2 tsp grated palm sugar or
   soft brown sugar

1 Chinese roasted duck
1 small red onion, thinly sliced
1 tbs julienned fresh ginger
4 tbs roughly chopped coriander
   (cilantro)
4 tbs roughly chopped mint
80 g (1/2 cup) roasted unsalted
   cashew nuts
8 butter lettuce leaves

To make the chilli dressing, put the chilli flakes in a frying pan and dry-fry over medium heat for 30 seconds, then grind to a powder in a mortar and pestle or spice grinder. Put the powder in a small bowl with the fish sauce, lime juice and sugar; mix well to dissolve the sugar and set aside.

Remove the flesh from the duck, cut it into bite-sized pieces and put it in a bowl. Add the onion, ginger, coriander, mint and cashews. Pour in the dressing and toss together gently.

Arrange the lettuce on a serving platter, or use the leaves to line individual serving bowls. Top with the duck salad and serve.

Serves 4

## prawn and fennel salad

1.25 kg (2 lb 12 oz) raw large
    prawns (shrimp), peeled
    and deveined
1 large fennel bulb (about
    400 g/14 oz), thinly sliced
300 g (10$^1$/$_2$ oz/$^1$/$_2$ large bunch)
    watercress, picked
2 tbs finely snipped chives

lemon and dijon dressing
3 tbs lemon juice
125 ml (4 fl oz/$^1$/$_2$ cup)
    extra virgin olive oil
1 tbs Dijon mustard
1 large garlic clove, finely
    chopped

Bring a large pot of water to the boil. Add the prawns, return to the boil and simmer for 2 minutes, or until the prawns turn pink and are cooked through. Drain and leave to cool. Pat the prawns dry with paper towels, slice them in half lengthways and put in a large serving bowl. Add the fennel, watercress and chives and mix well.

Whisk all the lemon and Dijon dressing ingredients together in a small bowl until well combined. Pour the dressing over the salad, season with salt and cracked black pepper and toss gently. Arrange the salad on four serving plates and serve at once.

Serves 4

Fennel brings its wonderfully astringent bite to this salad, lending an added piquancy to each forkful.

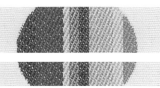

### cannellini bean salad with fennel and tuna

150 g (5$^1$/$_2$ oz/ $^3$/$_4$ cup) dried
   cannellini beans (see Note)
2 fresh bay leaves, torn
1 large garlic clove, smashed
235 g (8$^1$/$_2$ oz) green beans,
   trimmed
1 baby fennel bulb, thinly sliced
$^1$/$_2$ small red onion, finely sliced
1 handful parsley leaves, chopped
1 tbs olive oil
300 g (10$^1$/$_2$ oz) fresh tuna steaks

**lemon and chilli dressing**
3 tbs lemon juice
1 garlic clove, finely chopped
1 red chilli, seeded and finely
   chopped
$^1$/$_2$ tsp sugar
3 tsp lemon zest
4 tbs extra virgin olive oil

Put the cannellini beans in a bowl, cover with plenty of cold water and leave overnight, or for at least 8 hours. Rinse the beans well and put them in a large pot. Cover with plenty of cold water, add the bay leaves and garlic, bring to the boil, then reduce the heat and simmer for about 20–25 minutes, or until tender. Drain.

Meanwhile, bring another pot of lightly salted water to the boil, add the green beans and blanch until just tender, about 2–3 minutes. Drain, refresh under cold water, then drain again. Gently toss in a serving bowl with the fennel, onion and parsley.

Heat the oil in a large, heavy-based frying pan and cook the tuna steaks over high heat for 2 minutes on each side — they should still be pink in the centre. Remove from the pan and rest for 2–3 minutes. While the tuna is resting, whisk all the lemon and chilli dressing ingredients in a small bowl until well combined. Season with salt and pepper.

Cut the tuna into 3 cm (1 1/4 inch) chunks. Add to the green beans with the cannellini beans, pour the dressing over and gently toss to combine.

Note: To save time you can use a 400 g (14 oz) tin of cannellini beans instead of the dried beans. Leave out the first step and simply rinse and drain them well before adding them to the salad with the green beans.

Serves 4

roast duck salad with chilli dressing

## lentil salad

1/2 brown onion
2 cloves
300 g (10¹/2 oz/1²/3 cups)
   Puy or green lentils
1 strip lemon zest
2 garlic cloves, peeled
1 fresh bay leaf
2 tsp ground cumin

2 tbs red wine vinegar
3 tbs olive oil
1 tbs lemon juice
2 tbs finely chopped mint leaves
3 spring onions (scallions),
   finely chopped

Stud the onion with the cloves and put it in a pot with the lentils, lemon zest, garlic, bay leaf, 1 teaspoon of the cumin and 875 ml (32 fl oz/ 3¹/2 cups) water. Bring to the boil, then reduce the heat to medium and cook for 25–30 minutes, or until the water has been absorbed. Discard the onion, lemon zest and bay leaf, then finely chop the garlic cloves.

Put the chopped garlic in a bowl, add the vinegar, oil, lemon juice and remaining cumin and whisk together well. Stir the mixture through the lentils along with the mint and spring onion. Season well and leave for 30 minutes to let the flavours develop. Serve at room temperature.

Serves 4 as a side salad

## lamb, capsicum and cucumber salad

1 red onion, very thinly sliced
1 red capsicum (pepper),
    very thinly sliced
1 green capsicum (pepper),
    very thinly sliced
2 large Lebanese (short)
    cucumbers, cut into batons
4 tbs shredded mint

3 tbs chopped dill
oil, for brushing
600 g (1 lb 5 oz) lamb
    backstraps or loin fillets
4 tbs lemon juice
2 small garlic cloves, crushed
100 ml (3$^1$/2 fl oz) extra virgin
    olive oil

Toss the onion, the red and green capsicum, cucumber, mint and dill together in a large bowl.

Heat a chargrill pan (griddle) or frying pan to medium. Lightly brush with oil and cook the lamb for 2–3 minutes on each side, or until tender but still a little pink in the middle. Remove from the pan and allow to rest for 5 minutes. Thinly slice the lamb and gently mix it through the salad.

Combine the lemon juice and garlic in a small jug, then whisk in the oil with a fork until well combined. Season with salt and black pepper, then gently toss the dressing through the salad. Delicious served on fresh or toasted Turkish bread spread with hummus.

Serves 4

The sting of sweet heat, tender beef and fresh, zesty salad blow out the senses but not the waistline.

## thai beef salad

600 g (1 lb 5 oz) beef fillet, trimmed
2 tbs fish sauce
1 tbs peanut oil
2 vine-ripened tomatoes, each cut into 8 wedges
1/2 butter lettuce, leaves separated

**mint and chilli dressing**
1 small dried red chilli, roughly chopped
4 tbs fish sauce
4 red Asian shallots, finely sliced
2 spring onions (scallions), thinly sliced on the diagonal
4 tbs mint leaves
4 tbs coriander (cilantro) leaves
1 garlic clove, crushed
100 ml (3 1/2 fl oz) lime juice
2 tsp grated palm sugar or soft brown sugar

Put the beef in a bowl and pour over the fish sauce. Cover and refrigerate for 3 hours, turning the meat several times to coat.

Put a baking tray in the oven and preheat the oven to 220°C (425°F/Gas 7). Heat the oil in a frying pan and cook the beef fillet over high heat for 1 minute on each side, or until browned, then place on the hot baking tray and roast for 15 minutes for a medium-rare result. Remove from the oven, cover loosely with foil and allow to rest for 10 minutes.

Meanwhile, make the mint and chilli dressing. Put a small, non-stick frying pan over medium–high heat. Add the chilli and dry-fry for 1–2 minutes, or until dark but not burnt. Transfer to a mortar and pestle or spice mill and grind to a fine powder. Place in a bowl with the remaining dressing ingredients, stirring to dissolve the sugar.

Thinly slice the beef and toss in a bowl with the dressing and tomato. Arrange the lettuce on a serving platter and pile the beef salad on top. Serve warm.

Serves 4

thai beef salad

## green salad with lemon vinaigrette

1 baby cos (romaine) lettuce
1 small butter lettuce
30 g (1 oz/1 cup) picked
   watercress leaves
100 g (3 1/2 oz/1 small bunch)
   rocket (arugula), trimmed

**lemon vinaigrette**
2 tsp finely chopped French
   shallots (eschalots)

1 1/2 tsp Dijon mustard
pinch of sugar
3 tsp finely chopped basil
1/2 tsp grated lemon zest
2 tsp lemon juice
3 tsp white wine vinegar
3 tsp lemon oil or olive oil
2 1/2 tsp virgin olive oil

Separate all the lettuce leaves and rinse well. Rinse the watercress and rocket, then thoroughly drain all the salad greens. Pat dry and refrigerate.

To make the lemon vinaigrette, whisk the shallot, mustard, sugar, basil, lemon zest, lemon juice and vinegar in a bowl. Mix the lemon oil and olive oil in a small jug and slowly add to the dressing in a thin stream, whisking constantly to create a smooth, creamy dressing. Season to taste.

Put all the salad greens in a large bowl. Drizzle the dressing over the top, toss gently to coat and serve at once.

Serves 4 as a side salad

## tabbouleh

130 g (4½ oz/¾ cup) burghul
   (bulgar) wheat
80 g (2¾ oz/1 bunch) mint
200 g (7 oz/1 large bunch)
   flat-leaf (Italian) parsley
   (see Note)

4 spring onions (scallions),
   finely sliced
1 large tomato, finely chopped
2 garlic cloves, finely chopped
3 tbs lemon juice
4 tbs extra virgin olive oil

Put the burghul in a large bowl and add enough hot water to cover. Leave to soak for 15–20 minutes, or until tender. Drain well and thoroughly squeeze out all the excess liquid.

Finely chop the mint and parsley and toss in a large bowl with the burghul, spring onion and tomato.

Mix the garlic and lemon juice in a small jug. Whisk in the oil and season to taste. Toss the dressing through the salad and serve.

Note: To vary this recipe you could halve the quantity of parsley and add 100 g (3½ oz/1 small bunch) of rocket (arugula). To make the tabbouleh extra special, add 3 tablespoons of toasted pine nuts.

Serves 4 as a side salad

## crab salad with green mango and coconut

dressing
2 garlic cloves, peeled
1 small red chilli
1¹/2 tbs dried shrimp
1¹/2 tbs fish sauce
2 tbs lime juice
2 tsp palm sugar or soft
    brown sugar

4 tbs shredded coconut
    (see Note)
200 g (7 oz/2 cups) shredded
    green mango (see Note)
1 small handful mint leaves
    (torn if very big)

1 small handful coriander
    (cilantro) leaves
2 kaffir (makrut) lime leaves,
    shredded
1¹/2 tsp thinly shredded pickled
    ginger
350 g (12 oz) fresh crab meat
4 small squares banana leaves
    (optional)
50 g (1³/4 oz/¹/3 cup) chopped
    toasted unsalted peanuts
4 lime wedges

Preheat the oven to 180°C (350°F/Gas 4). To make the dressing, pound the garlic, chilli, dried shrimp and ¹/2 teaspoon salt to a paste in a mortar and pestle. Whisk in the fish sauce, lime juice and sugar with a fork.

Spread the shredded coconut on a baking tray and bake for 1–2 minutes, shaking the tray occasionally to ensure even toasting. Watch the coconut closely, as it will burn easily.

Put the shredded mango in a large bowl and add the mint, coriander, lime leaves, ginger, coconut and crab meat. Pour the dressing over the top and toss together gently.

If using the banana leaves, place a square in each serving bowl (the leaves are for presentation only and are not edible). Mound some crab salad on top, sprinkle with the peanuts and serve immediately with lime wedges.

Note: Freshly shredded coconut is delicious, so if you have the time, remove the skin from a coconut and shred the flesh using a vegetable peeler. For this recipe you will need about 3 green mangoes to get the right quantity of shredded mango flesh.

Serves 4

crab salad with green mango and coconut

## chargrilled tomato salad

8 Roma (plum) tomatoes
1$\frac{1}{2}$ tsp capers, rinsed and drained
4 basil leaves, torn
3 tsp olive oil
3 tsp balsamic vinegar
1 garlic clove, crushed
$\frac{1}{4}$ tsp honey

Cut the tomatoes lengthways into quarters and scoop out the seeds. Heat a chargrill pan (griddle) to medium and cook the tomato quarters for 1–2 minutes on each side, or until grill marks appear and the tomatoes have softened. Cool to room temperature and place in a bowl.

Combine the capers, basil, oil, vinegar, garlic and honey in a small bowl and season with salt and freshly ground black pepper. Pour the mixture over the tomatoes and toss together gently. Serve at room temperature with crusty bread and grilled meats.

Serves 4 as a side salad

## south-western black bean salad

165 g (5³/4 oz/³/4 cup) dried
   black (turtle) beans
150 g (5¹/2 oz/³/4 cup) dried
   cannellini beans
1 small red onion, chopped
1 small red capsicum (pepper),
   chopped
265 g (9¹/2 oz/1¹/3 cups) tinned
   corn kernels, drained

3 tbs chopped coriander
   (cilantro)

### dressing

1 garlic clove, crushed
¹/2 tsp ground cumin
¹/2 tsp French mustard
2 tbs red wine vinegar
3 tbs olive oil

Put the black beans and cannellini beans in separate bowls, cover with plenty of cold water and leave to soak overnight. Rinse well, then drain and place in separate pots and cover with water. Bring both pots of water to the boil, reduce the heat and simmer for 45 minutes, or until the beans are tender. Drain, rinse and allow to cool, then put all the beans in a serving bowl. Mix through the onion, capsicum, corn and coriander.

To make the dressing, combine the garlic, cumin, mustard and vinegar in a small jug, then gradually whisk in the oil. Season lightly with salt and pepper. Pour over the bean mixture, toss lightly to combine and serve.

Serves 4 as a side salad

Bathing the cucumber in a warm marinade imparts a tenderness rarely associated with this cool, crispy customer.

## beef teriyaki with cucumber salad

4 beef fillet steaks (about
   180 g/6 oz each)
4 tbs soy sauce
2 tbs mirin
1 tbs sake (optional)
1 garlic clove, crushed
1 tsp grated fresh ginger
oil, for brushing
1 tsp sugar
1 tsp toasted sesame seeds

cucumber salad
1 large Lebanese (short)
   cucumber, peeled, seeded
   and diced
1/2 red capsicum (pepper), diced
2 spring onions (scallions), sliced
   thinly on the diagonal
2 tsp sugar
1 tbs rice wine vinegar

Put the beef steaks side by side in a large dish. Combine the soy sauce, mirin, sake, garlic and ginger and pour over the steaks, turning to coat. Cover and refrigerate for at least 30 minutes, turning once or twice.

To make the cucumber salad, toss the cucumber, capsicum and spring onion in a bowl. Put the sugar and rice wine vinegar in a saucepan with 3 tablespoons of water and stir over medium heat until the sugar has dissolved. Increase the heat and simmer for 3–4 minutes, or until the mixture has thickened. Pour over the cucumber salad, stir to combine and leave to cool completely.

Heat a chargrill pan (griddle) or barbecue hotplate to high and brush with a little oil. Drain the beef fillets, reserving the marinade. Cook the fillets for 4 minutes on each side, or until done to your liking. Remove from the heat, cover with foil and rest in a warm place for 5–10 minutes.

Put the sugar and the reserved marinade in a saucepan and heat, stirring, until the sugar has dissolved. Bring to the boil and simmer for 2 minutes. Take off the heat, but keep warm.

Slice each fillet into 1 cm ($1/2$ inch) strips and arrange on four serving plates. Spoon some of the marinade and cucumber salad over the top and sprinkle with the sesame seeds. Serve with steamed rice.

Serves 4

chargrilled tomato salad

## chickpea and olive salad

330 g (10$^{1/2}$ oz/1$^{1/2}$ cups)
   dried chickpeas
1 Lebanese (short) cucumber
2 tomatoes, seeded and cut
   into 1 cm ($^{1/2}$ inch) cubes
1 small red onion, finely chopped
3 tbs chopped parsley
60 g (2$^{1/4}$ oz/$^{1/2}$ cup) pitted
   black olives

**lemon and garlic dressing**
1 tbs lemon juice
3 tbs olive oil
1 garlic clove, crushed
1 tsp runny honey

Cover the chickpeas in plenty of cold water and leave to soak overnight. Drain well, put them in a pot and cover with cold water. Bring to the boil, then reduce the heat to a fast simmer and cook for 25 minutes, or until just tender. Drain and allow to cool, then place in a serving bowl.

Cut the cucumber in half lengthways, scoop out the seeds and cut the flesh into 1 cm ($^{1/2}$ inch) chunks. Add to the chickpeas with the tomato, onion, parsley and olives. Put all the lemon and garlic dressing ingredients in a small screw-top jar, shake well and pour over the salad. Toss lightly to combine and serve at room temperature.

Serves 4 as a side salad

## salata baladi

1¹/₂ tbs extra virgin olive oil
1¹/₂ tbs lemon juice
1 baby cos (romaine) lettuce, leaves torn
2 ripe tomatoes, each cut into 8 wedges
1 small green capsicum (pepper), cut into bite-sized pieces

2 small Lebanese (short) cucumbers, seeded and chopped
4 radishes, sliced
1 small salad or red onion, thinly sliced (see Note)
2 tbs chopped flat-leaf (Italian) parsley
1 small handful mint leaves

In a bowl, whisk together the oil and lemon juice. Season well with salt and freshly cracked black pepper.

Put all the vegetables and herbs in a large serving bowl and toss together well. Add the dressing and toss again. Serve at once, while the salad is crisp.

Note: Salad onions are sweeter than normal onions. Ask your greengrocer if you are unsure which ones to buy.

Serves 4 as a side salad

The simplest lemon vinaigrette and a scattering of parsley bring out the true, sweet flavour of superbly fresh seafood.

## seafood salad

500 g (1 lb 2 oz) small squid
1 kg (2 lb 4 oz) large clams (vongole)
1 kg (2 lb 4 oz) black mussels
500 g (1 lb 2 oz) raw prawns (shrimp), peeled and deveined, tails intact

2 handfuls flat-leaf (Italian) parsley, finely chopped

dressing
2 tbs lemon juice
4 tbs olive oil
1 garlic clove, crushed

To clean the squid, gently pull the tentacles away from the hoods (the intestines should come away at the same time). Remove the intestines from the tentacles by cutting under the eyes, then remove the beak if it remains in the centre of the tentacles by using your fingers to push up the centre. Pull away the soft bones (quill) from the hoods. Rub the hoods under cold running water and the skin should come away easily. Rinse well, then slice the squid into rings and roughly chop the tentacles.

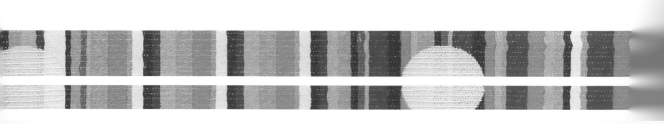

Scrub the clams and mussels with a stiff brush and pull out the hairy beards. Discard any that are cracked, or open ones that don't close when tapped on the bench. Rinse well under running water. Fill a pot with 2 cm (3/4 inch) of water and add the clams and mussels. Cover and boil for 4–5 minutes, or until the shells open. Remove, reserving the liquid, and discard any that do not open. Remove the mussels and clams from their shells and place them in a bowl.

Bring 1 litre (35 fl oz/4 cups) of water to the boil, then add the prawns and squid. Simmer for 3–4 minutes, or until the prawns turn pink and the squid is tender. Drain and add to the clams and mussels.

In a small bowl, whisk all the dressing ingredients together. Season to taste and pour over the seafood. Add 4 tablespoons of the parsley, gently toss to coat, then cover and refrigerate for 30–40 minutes. Just before serving, sprinkle with the remaining parsley.

Serves 4

salata baladi

## citrus, sugar snap pea and walnut salad

2 oranges

2 small grapefruit

100 g (3¹/2 oz) sugar snap peas

75 g (2¹/2 oz/¹/2 bunch) rocket
   (arugula), leaves torn

¹/2 oak leaf lettuce, leaves torn

1 Lebanese (short) cucumber,
   sliced

4 tbs walnut pieces

### walnut dressing

2 tbs walnut oil

2 tbs oil

2 tsp tarragon vinegar

2 tsp seeded mustard

1 tsp sweet chilli sauce

Peel the rind and bitter white pith from the oranges and grapefruit. Cut the flesh into segments between the membranes, removing the seeds. Place the segments in a large serving bowl.

Trim the sugar snap peas, put them in a pot and cover with boiling water. Leave to stand for 2 minutes, then refresh under cold water. Drain and pat dry with paper towels and add to the citrus segments with the rocket, lettuce, cucumber and walnut pieces.

Put all the walnut dressing ingredients in a screw-top jar and shake well to combine. Pour the dressing over the salad, toss well and serve.

Serves 4 as a side salad

## prawn and papaya salad with lime dressing

750 g (1 lb 10 oz) cooked
    prawns (shrimp)
1 large papaya, peeled, seeded
    and chopped
1 small red onion, finely sliced
2 celery stalks, finely sliced
2 tbs shredded mint

### lime dressing
125 ml (4 fl oz/ 1/2 cup) oil
3 tbs lime juice
2 tsp finely grated fresh ginger
1 tsp caster (superfine) sugar

Peel the prawns, leaving the tails intact. Gently pull out the dark vein from each prawn back, starting at the head end. Put the prawns in a bowl.

Whisk all the lime dressing ingredients together in a small bowl. Season to taste with salt and freshly ground black pepper, then pour over the prawns and gently toss to coat. Add the papaya, onion, celery and mint and gently toss to combine. Serve the salad at room temperature, or cover and refrigerate for up to 3 hours before serving.

Serves 4

Poaching squid in a fragrant broth scented with lemon grass and lime leaves renders it delicate, tender and aromatic.

## squid salad

**lime and ginger dressing**
2 large garlic cloves, crushed
2 tsp grated fresh ginger
3 small red chillies, seeded
    and thinly sliced
2 tbs grated palm sugar or
    soft brown sugar
2 tbs fish sauce
2 tbs lime juice
1/2 tsp sesame oil

500 g (1 lb 2 oz) cleaned squid
    tubes
6 makrut (kaffir lime) leaves
1 stem lemon grass, white part
    only, chopped
3–4 red Asian shallots, thinly sliced
1 Lebanese (short) cucumber,
    cut in half lengthways,
    seeded and thinly sliced
3 tbs chopped coriander
    (cilantro) leaves
4 tbs mint leaves
fried red Asian shallot flakes,
    to serve

Put the lime and ginger dressing ingredients in a small pan with 1 tablespoon of water. Stir over low heat until the sugar has dissolved. Set aside.

Cut the squid tubes in half lengthways and rinse under running water. Score a criss-cross pattern on the inside of the squid, taking care not to cut all the way through, then cut the squid into 3 cm (1 1/4 inch) pieces.

Put the lime leaves and lemon grass in a pot with 1.25 litres (44 fl oz/5 cups) water. Bring to the boil, reduce the heat and simmer for 5 minutes. Add half the squid and cook for 30 seconds, or until they begin to curl up and turn opaque. Remove with a slotted spoon and keep warm. Repeat with the remaining squid, then discard the liquid, lime leaves and lemon grass.

Put the squid, shallot, cucumber, coriander, mint and lettuce in a large bowl, then add the dressing and toss together well. Scatter with the fried shallot flakes and serve.

Serves 4

squid salad

## escabeche

500 g (1 lb 2 oz) skinless fish
    fillets, such as red mullet,
    whiting, redfish or garfish
seasoned plain (all-purpose)
    flour
100 ml (3$^{1}$/2 fl oz) extra virgin
    olive oil
1 red onion, thinly sliced
2 garlic cloves, thinly sliced
2 thyme sprigs

1 tsp ground cumin
2 spring onions (scallions), sliced
$^{1}$/2 tsp finely grated orange zest
3 tbs orange juice
185 ml (6 fl oz/$^{3}$/4 cup) white wine
185 ml (6 fl oz/$^{3}$/4 cup) white
    wine vinegar
60 g (2 oz/$^{1}$/2 cup) pitted green
    olives, roughly chopped
$^{1}$/2 tsp caster (superfine) sugar

Dust the fish lightly with the flour. Heat 2 tablespoons of the oil in a frying pan over medium heat and cook the fish in batches for 2–3 minutes on each side, or until lightly browned and cooked through. Place in a single layer in a large, shallow, non-metallic dish.

Heat the remaining oil in the same pan. Add the onion and garlic and cook, stirring, over medium heat for 5 minutes, or until soft. Add the thyme, cumin and spring onion and stir until fragrant, then add the remaining ingredients and season to taste. Bring to the boil, then pour the liquid over the fish. Allow the fish to cool in the liquid, or refrigerate overnight. Serve at room temperature, on a bed of watercress or salad greens.

Serves 4

## scallop ceviche

16 scallops, on the half-shell
1 tsp finely grated lime zest,
    plus extra strips of lime
    zest, to serve
2 garlic cloves, chopped

2 small red chillies, seeded and
    finely chopped
125 ml (4 fl oz/1/2 cup) lime juice
1–2 tbs chopped parsley
1 tbs olive oil

Remove the scallops from their shells and reserve the shells. You may need to use a small, sharp knife to slice the scallops free — be careful not to leave any scallop meat behind. Slice or pull off any vein, membrane or hard white muscle, leaving any roe attached. Rinse the scallops and pat them dry with paper towels.

In a large non-metallic bowl, mix together the remaining ingredients and season with salt and freshly ground black pepper. Add the scallops and gently stir to coat. Cover with plastic wrap and refrigerate for 2 hours, or up to 1 day — during this time the acid in the lime juice will 'cook' the scallops, firming the flesh and turning it opaque.

To serve, slide each scallop back onto a half-shell and spoon the dressing over. Scatter with lime zest strips and enjoy cold as a starter salad.

Serves 4

When the occasion calls for a bit of flair, this salad has all the flashiness of flamenco and sings of siestas in the sun.

### spanish-style seafood salad

500 g (1 lb 2 oz) raw prawns (shrimp)
150 g (5½ oz) scallops, with roe
12 black mussels
2 slices of lemon
2 fresh or dried bay leaves
pinch of dried thyme
200 g (7 oz) broccoli, cut into small florets
2 tsp capers, rinsed and drained
16 dry-cured black olives

2 spring onions (scallions), chopped
½ small green capsicum (pepper), diced

dressing
2 tbs olive oil
1½ tbs lemon juice
1 tsp Dijon mustard
1 garlic clove, crushed

Peel the prawns and pull out the dark vein from each prawn back, starting at the head end. Slice or pull off any vein, membrane or hard white muscle from the scallops, leaving any roe attached. Rinse the scallops and pat them dry with paper towels.

Scrub the mussels with a stiff brush and pull out the hairy beards. Discard any broken mussels, or open ones that don't close when tapped on the bench. Rinse well under running water.

Put the lemon slices, bay leaves and thyme in a large pot with 750 ml (24 fl oz/3 cups) water. Bring to the boil. Add the scallops and cook for 30 seconds, or until opaque. Remove with a slotted spoon and drain on crumpled paper towels. Add the prawns and cook for 2–3 minutes, or until opaque. Remove with a slotted spoon and drain on paper towels.

Add the mussels to the pan, cover and cook for 4–5 minutes, or until they open, shaking the pan occasionally. Drain the mussels on crumpled paper towels, discarding any that haven't opened. Discard one half-shell from each mussel and put all the seafood in a serving bowl.

Blanch the broccoli in a pot of boiling water for 2 minutes. Refresh in cold water, then drain and add to the seafood with the capers, olives, spring onion and capsicum.

Whisk the dressing ingredients in a bowl with some salt and freshly ground black pepper. Pour over the seafood and gently toss to coat. Cover and refrigerate for about 2 hours before serving.

Serves 4

scallop ceviche

## smoked trout with chilli raspberry dressing

160 g (5³/4 oz/2 bunches) sorrel
1 small smoked trout
12 asparagus spears, trimmed
1 small red onion, thinly sliced
200 g (7 oz) pear tomatoes,
   halved
150 g (5¹/2 oz/1 punnet)
   raspberries

**chilli raspberry dressing**
100 g (3¹/2 oz/²/3 punnet)
   raspberries
1/2 tsp chilli paste
1 garlic clove, crushed
4 tbs olive oil
1¹/2 tbs raspberry vinegar
   or white wine vinegar

Trim the stalks from the sorrel, rinse the leaves well, pat them dry and put in the refrigerator to crisp. Peel away and discard the skin and bones from the trout. Break the flesh into pieces.

Put the chilli raspberry dressing ingredients in a small pan over low heat until the raspberries begin to break up and colour the liquid. Transfer to a bowl, whisk well and season with salt and freshly ground black pepper.

Boil, steam or microwave the asparagus until just tender, then drain and refresh under cold water. Drain again. Divide the sorrel between individual plates. Arrange the asparagus, trout, onion, tomatoes and raspberries on top, drizzle with the dressing and serve.

Serves 4

# roast cherry tomato and chicken salad

250 g (9 oz/1 punnet) cherry
tomatoes or small truss
tomatoes
2 whole garlic cloves, unpeeled
1 tbs olive oil
1 thyme sprig, cut into 3 pieces

1 barbecued chicken
100 g (3½ oz) baby rocket
(arugula) leaves
2 tbs capers, rinsed and drained
(optional)
1 tbs balsamic vinegar

Preheat the oven to 180°C (350°F/Gas 4). Put the tomatoes, whole garlic cloves, oil and thyme in a roasting tin and bake for 15 minutes.

Meanwhile, remove the meat from the chicken, discarding the skin and bones. Shred the meat and toss in a bowl with the rocket and capers.

Allow the cooked tomatoes to cool slightly, then gently squash each one to release some of the juice. Add the tomatoes to the chicken mixture, leaving the garlic and pan juices in the roasting dish. Discard the thyme. Squeeze the flesh from each roasted garlic clove and mix with any pan juices. Add the vinegar and mix again. Pour the mixture over the salad, toss gently and serve.

Serves 4

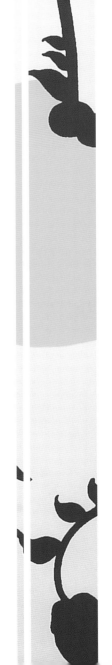

A deeply satisfying dish that is a treat for the lips and kind to the hips, and healthy through and through.

## brown rice and puy lentils with pine nuts and spinach

135 g (5 oz/2/3 cup) brown rice
3 tbs extra virgin olive oil
1 small red onion, diced
2 garlic cloves, crushed
1 small carrot, diced
1 1/2 celery stalks, diced
125 g (4 1/2 oz/2/3 cup) Puy
    lentils (see Note)
2 small tomatoes, seeded
    and diced

2 tbs chopped coriander
    (cilantro)
2 tbs chopped mint
1 1/2 tbs balsamic vinegar
3 tsp lemon juice
2 tbs toasted pine nuts
100 g (3 1/2 oz/2 heaped cups)
    baby English spinach leaves

Bring a large pot of water to the boil. Add 1 teaspoon of salt and the rice, then cook for 20 minutes, or until tender. Drain well, then rinse the rice under cold running water.

Heat 2 tablespoons of the oil in a saucepan and fry the onion, garlic, carrot and celery over low heat for 5 minutes, or until softened. Add the lentils and 375 ml (13 fl oz/1$^{1}/_{2}$ cups) of water. Bring to the boil, then reduce the heat and simmer for 15 minutes, or until tender. Drain well, but do not rinse. Place in a large bowl with the rice, tomato, coriander and mint.

Whisk the remaining oil with the vinegar and lemon juice and season well with salt and freshly ground black pepper. Pour the dressing over the lentils, add the pine nuts and spinach, toss well and serve.

Note: Puy lentils are green French lentils available at specialist food stores and some supermarkets. If you are unable to obtain any, you can use green or brown lentils instead.

Serves 4 as a side salad

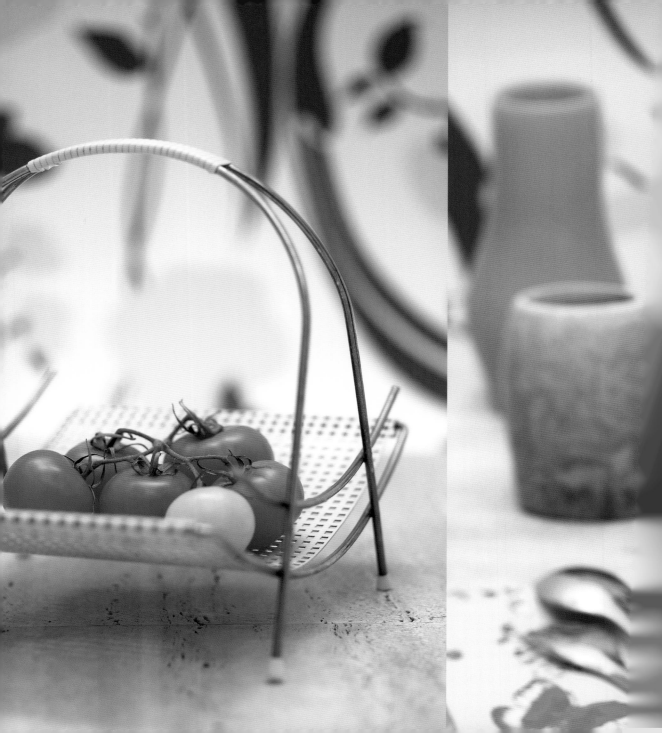

roast cherry tomato and chicken salad

## thai noodle salad

250 g (9 oz) dried instant
    egg noodles
500 g (1 lb 2 oz) cooked large
    prawns (shrimp), peeled
    and deveined, tails intact
5 spring onions (scallions), sliced
2 tbs chopped coriander
    (cilantro)
1 red capsicum (pepper), diced
100 g (3¹/2 oz) snowpeas
    (mangetout), julienned
4 lime wedges

### dressing

2 tbs grated fresh ginger
2 tbs soy sauce
2 tbs sesame oil
4 tbs red wine vinegar
1 tbs sweet chilli sauce
2 garlic cloves, crushed
4 tbs kecap manis

Cook the egg noodles in a pot of boiling water for 2 minutes, or until tender. Drain thoroughly, then leave to cool in a large serving bowl.

Whisk all the dressing ingredients together in a bowl and gently mix through the cooled noodles. Add the prawns, spring onion, coriander, capsicum and snowpeas. Toss gently and serve with lime wedges.

Serves 4

## marinated fish salad with chilli and basil

500 g (1 lb 2 oz) skinless firm
   white fish fillets
3 tbs lime juice
3 tbs light coconut milk
mixed salad leaves, to serve
3 tomatoes, diced
3 Lebanese (short) cucumbers,
   diced

5 spring onions (scallions),
   finely sliced
2 red chillies, seeded and sliced
2 garlic cloves, crushed
1 tsp grated fresh ginger
1 large handful basil leaves,
   chopped

Slice the fish into thin strips and place in a non-metallic bowl. Put the lime juice and coconut milk in a jug with 1 teaspoon salt and $1/4$ teaspoon of cracked black pepper. Mix well, then pour over the fish. Cover and refrigerate for several hours or overnight, turning once or twice. (The acid in the lime juice will 'cook' the fish, firming the flesh and turning it opaque.)

Arrange some salad leaves on four serving plates. Gently mix the tomato, cucumber, spring onion, chilli, garlic and ginger through the fish, spoon over the salad leaves and serve.

Note: When mangoes are in season, peel and roughly dice the flesh and toss it through the finished salad for extra flavour and sweetness.

Serves 4

The toasty, exotic allure of sesame always promises good food to come. These noodles are light yet utterly ravishing.

somen noodle salad with sesame dressing

sesame dressing
3 tbs toasted sesame seeds
2$1/2$ tbs shoyu or light soy sauce
2 tbs rice vinegar
2 tsp sugar
$1/2$ tsp grated fresh ginger
$1/2$ tsp dashi granules

125 g (4$1/2$ oz) dried somen
    noodles
100 g (3$1/2$ oz) snowpeas
    (mangetout), tailed and
    finely sliced on the diagonal
100 g (3$1/2$ oz/1 cup) julienned
    daikon radish
1 small carrot, julienned
1 spring onion (scallion), sliced
    on the diagonal
50 g (1$3/4$ oz/1 heaped cup) baby
    English spinach leaves
2 tsp toasted sesame seeds

To make the sesame dressing, put the sesame seeds in a mortar and pestle and grind until fine and moist. Combine the soy sauce, vinegar, sugar, ginger and dashi granules in a small saucepan with 125 ml (4 fl oz/$^1$/$_2$ cup) water and bring to the boil. Reduce the heat to medium and simmer, stirring, for 2 minutes, or until the dashi granules have dissolved. Remove from the heat and leave to cool. Gradually mix in the ground sesame seeds, stirring to form a thick dressing.

Cook the noodles in a large pot of boiling water for 2 minutes, or until tender. Drain, rinse under cold water and allow to cool completely. Cut the noodles into 10 cm (4 inch) lengths using scissors.

Put the snowpeas in a large shallow serving bowl with the daikon, carrot, spring onion, spinach and noodles. Add the dressing and toss well to combine, then cover and refrigerate until ready to serve. Just before serving, sprinkle with the toasted sesame seeds.

Serves 4

thai noodle salad

## garden salad

½ green oakleaf lettuce
150 g (5½ oz/1 bunch) rocket
   (arugula), trimmed
1 small radicchio lettuce
1 green capsicum (pepper),
   cut into thin strips
zest of 1 lemon

dressing
1 tbs roughly chopped coriander
   (cilantro)
1½ tbs lemon juice
1 tsp soft brown sugar
1 tbs olive oil
1 garlic clove, crushed (optional)

Wash and dry the salad greens thoroughly, then tear into bite-sized pieces.
Toss in a large serving bowl with the capsicum and lemon zest.

Whisk the dressing ingredients in a small mixing bowl until the sugar has
dissolved. Just before serving, pour the dressing over the salad and toss well.

Serves 4 as a side salad

## borlotti bean, beetroot and mint salad

400 g (14 oz) tin borlotti beans,
    drained and rinsed (see Note)
450 g (1 lb) tin baby beetroot,
    drained and chopped
150 g (5$^1$/$_2$ oz) cherry tomatoes,
    halved
1 handful mint leaves

dressing
1 tbs apple cider vinegar or
    white wine vinegar
1 tbs olive oil

Put the beans, beetroot and cherry tomatoes in a serving dish. Roughly chop half the mint leaves and mix them through the salad. Whisk the dressing ingredients in a small bowl and season to taste. Pour over the salad and mix gently. Scatter over the remaining mint leaves and serve.

Note: When available, use fresh borlotti beans in this recipe. First blanch them in a pot of boiling water for several minutes until tender.

Serves 4 as a side salad

## pork noodle salad

stock
250 ml (9 fl oz/1 cup)
    chicken stock
3 coriander (cilantro) roots
2 makrut (kaffir lime) leaves
3 x 3 cm (1¼ x 1¼ inch) piece
    of fresh ginger, peeled
    and sliced

dressing
3 tbs lime juice
3 tbs fish sauce
1½ tbs palm sugar or soft
    brown sugar
¼ tsp ground white pepper

30 g (1 oz) fresh black fungus
    (wood ears)
100 g (3½ oz) dried rice vermicelli
1 small red chilli, seeded and
    finely sliced, plus extra,
    to serve
2 red Asian shallots, finely sliced
2 spring onions (scallions),
    finely sliced
2 garlic cloves, crushed
250 g (9 oz) minced (ground) pork
1 handful coriander (cilantro)
    leaves, chopped, plus extra
    whole leaves, to serve
8 oakleaf or coral lettuce leaves,
    torn or shredded
4 lime wedges

To make the stock, put the chicken stock, coriander roots, lime leaves and ginger in a saucepan with 250 ml (9 fl oz/1 cup) water and bring to the boil. Reduce the heat and simmer for about 25 minutes, or until reduced to 185 ml (6 fl oz/3/4 cup). Strain, return to the saucepan and set aside.

Combine the dressing ingredients in a small bowl, stirring until the sugar has dissolved. Set aside until needed.

Discard the woody stems from the fungus, then thinly slice the caps. Soak the vermicelli in warm water for 5 minutes. Drain well, then cut into 3 cm (1¼ inch) lengths. Gently toss in a bowl with the fungus, chilli, shallot, spring onion and garlic.

Return the stock to the heat and bring to the boil. Add the pork and stir, breaking up any lumps, for 1–2 minutes, or until the pork changes colour and is cooked through. Drain, then add to the vermicelli mixture with the dressing and chopped coriander. Mix well, then season to taste.

Arrange the lettuce on a serving platter and spoon the pork mixture over the top. Scatter with the extra chilli slices and whole coriander leaves and serve with the lime wedges.

Serves 4

borlotti bean, beetroot and mint salad

## smoked salmon and fennel salad

**dressing**
2 tsp Dijon mustard
1 tsp caster (superfine) sugar
125 ml (4 fl oz/1/2 cup) olive oil
2 tbs lemon juice

2 fennel bulbs, thinly sliced,
   fronds reserved (see Note)
200 g (7 oz) smoked salmon,
   cut into strips
2 tbs snipped chives
rocket (arugula) leaves, to serve
4 lemon wedges

Thoroughly whisk all the dressing ingredients together in a large bowl.

Chop enough reserved fennel fronds to fill a tablespoon and add to the dressing with the sliced fennel, smoked salmon and chives. Season with salt and pepper and toss gently. Arrange some rocket leaves on four serving plates and pile the salad on top. Serve with the lemon wedges and perhaps some crusty bread.

Note: You could use a tablespoon of chopped fresh dill in place of the fennel fronds in this recipe.

Serves 4

# hawaiian poke salad

5 g (¹/₈ oz) dried wakame
   (curly-leaved seaweed)
500 g (1 lb 2 oz) fish steaks,
   such as tuna or swordfish
1 large onion, finely chopped
6 spring onions (scallions),
   finely sliced

2 small red chillies, cut
   into thin strips
4 tbs low-salt soy sauce
1 tbs sesame oil
4–6 lettuce leaves
1 tbs sesame seeds, toasted
4 lime wedges

Soak the wakame in a bowl of cold water for 15 minutes. Drain well.

Cut the fish into small cubes and place in a non-metallic bowl with the wakame, onion, spring onion, chilli, soy sauce and sesame oil. Cover and refrigerate for 4 hours.

Line a serving platter with lettuce leaves. Top with the marinated fish and sprinkle with the toasted sesame seeds. Serve with lime wedges.

Serves 4

Studded with salty olives, crispy prosciutto and cool sweet mint, every mouthful is a joy — a sensation in a bowl.

## fennel and crispy prosciutto salad

sherry vinegar dressing
2 tbs sherry vinegar
3 tbs olive oil

2 small fennel bulbs
2 Lebanese (short) cucumbers

100 g (3$^1$/$_2$ oz/$^3$/$_4$ cup) small
    whole black olives
6 slices of prosciutto, chopped
1 handful mint leaves

First, make the sherry vinegar dressing. Whisk the vinegar and oil in a small bowl and season with a little salt and black pepper. Set aside.

Next, prepare the fennel. Slice off and discard the feathery fronds and stalks from the top of the bulbs. Discard the outer layer from each fennel bulb, then cut a thin slice from the bottom of each bulb to form a flat base. Sit the fennel upright on a chopping board and very thinly slice it. Transfer the slices to a bowl and pour over two-thirds of the dressing. Toss well and leave to marinate for 2 hours, or up to 4 hours.

Slice the cucumbers in half lengthways and scoop out the seeds using a teaspoon. Chop again at about 1 cm ($1/2$ inch) intervals and put the cucumber slices in a serving dish with the olives.

Put a frying pan over high heat. When the pan is hot, add the prosciutto and dry-fry until crispy, about 2 minutes. Remove from the pan, leave to cool a little and cut into strips.

Add the fennel with all its marinade to the cucumber and olives. Pour over the remaining dressing and toss well. Top with the crispy prosciutto and mint leaves and serve.

Serves 4 as a side salad

fennel and crispy prosciutto salad

## tropical sprout salad

1 small pawpaw
2 tbs lime juice
50 g (1³/4 oz/¹/2 punnet) snowpea (mangetout) sprouts
2 small kiwifruit, peeled and thinly sliced
35 g (1¹/4 oz/¹/2 cup) alfalfa sprouts

Peel the pawpaw, cut it in half and scoop out the seeds. Cut the flesh into 1 cm (¹/2 inch) slices and arrange in a single layer on a board or plate. Drizzle with the lime juice and allow to sit for 10 minutes.

Arrange half the pawpaw slices in a layer in a serving bowl, then half the snowpea sprouts, half the kiwifruit slices and half the alfalfa sprouts. Repeat with the remaining ingredients and serve at once.

Serves 4 as a side salad

## semi-dried tomato and baby spinach salad

1 preserved lemon quarter
100 g (3$^1/_2$ oz/2 heaped cups) baby English spinach leaves
3–4 marinated artichoke hearts, drained and quartered
60 g (2$^1/_4$ oz/$^1/_3$ cup) small black olives
150 g (5$^1/_2$ oz) semi-dried (sun-blushed) tomatoes, sliced
1$^1/_2$ tbs lemon juice
2 tbs olive oil
1 large garlic clove, crushed

Remove the flesh from the preserved lemon. Rinse the rind thoroughly under running water, then drain well and thinly slice it. Toss in a serving bowl with the spinach, artichoke, olives and tomato.

Put the lemon juice, oil and garlic in a small bowl. Season and mix well, then pour over the salad and toss to coat. Serve immediately.

Serves 4 as a side salad

Tender young spring vegetables are a gift of nature and are at their best in this delicate salad with its zesty dressing.

## chicken and spring vegetable salad

600 g (1 lb 5 oz) chicken breast
    fillets
1/2 lime, juiced
4 kaffir (makrut) lime leaves,
    shredded
1/2 onion, peeled
6 black peppercorns
175 g (6 oz/1 bunch) asparagus

175 g (6 oz/1¼ cups) broad (fava)
    beans, defrosted if frozen
225 g (8 oz) baby green beans

lemon tarragon dressing
1 tbs olive oil
2 tbs lemon juice
2 tbs chopped tarragon leaves

Half-fill a large pot with water. Add the chicken, lime juice, lime leaves, onion and peppercorns. Cover and bring slowly to the boil, then reduce the heat and simmer for 3 minutes. Turn off the heat and leave the chicken to cool in the broth for at least 30 minutes — it will continue to cook during this time.

Meanwhile, combine the lemon tarragon dressing ingredients in a small bowl. Season lightly with salt and pepper, mix well and set aside.

Snap the woody ends off the asparagus and discard. Bring another pot of water to the boil and add a pinch of salt. Add the broad beans and cook for 1 minute, then add the green beans and simmer for 1 minute. Now add the asparagus and cook for another minute. Drain well and refresh under cold water. Drain well again.

Slice the asparagus spears lengthways and place them in a serving dish with the green beans. Remove the skins from the broad beans and add the beans to the serving dish.

Remove the cooled chicken from the poaching liquid. Shred the fillets, then gently toss them through the salad with the dressing. Serve at once.

Serves 4

chicken and spring vegetable salad

## moroccan carrot salad with green olives and mint

**harissa dressing**
1¹/₂ tsp cumin seeds
¹/₂ tsp coriander seeds
1 tbs red wine vinegar
2 tbs olive oil
1 garlic clove, crushed
2 tsp harissa
¹/₄ tsp orange flower water

600 g (1 lb 5 oz) baby (Dutch)
    carrots, tops trimmed,
    well scrubbed
8 large green olives, pitted
    and finely sliced
2 tbs shredded mint
30 g (1 oz/1 cup) picked
    watercress leaves

To make the harissa dressing, dry-fry the cumin and coriander seeds in a small frying pan over medium heat for 30 seconds, or until fragrant. Allow to cool, then grind in a mortar and pestle or spice grinder. Place in a large mixing bowl with the remaining dressing ingredients and whisk well.

Blanch the carrots in a pot of boiling salted water for 5 minutes, or until almost tender. Drain into a colander and allow to dry for a few minutes. While the carrots are still hot, gently swirl them about in the harissa dressing until nicely coated. Allow to cool to room temperature.

Add the olives and mint to the infused carrots, season well and toss gently to combine. Serve on a bed of watercress leaves.

Serves 4 as a side salad

## cherry and pear tomato salad with white beans

3 tbs olive oil
2 red Asian shallots, finely diced
1 large garlic clove, crushed
1½ tbs lemon juice
250 g (9 oz/1 punnet) cherry
    tomatoes, halved
250 g (9 oz/1 punnet) yellow
    pear tomatoes, halved

425 g (15 oz) tin white beans,
    drained and rinsed
1 large handful basil leaves,
    roughly torn
2 tbs chopped parsley

Put the oil, shallot, garlic and lemon juice in a small bowl and whisk well.

Put all the tomatoes in a serving bowl with the white beans. Drizzle with the shallot dressing and scatter the basil and parsley over the top. Toss together gently and serve.

Serves 4 as a side dish

Here, chargrilled chicken gets a smoky, spicy edge, brightened with a lemony yoghurt dressing for extra verve and pizazz.

## chargrilled chicken and sprout salad

600 g (1 lb 5 oz) chicken breast fillets
1 tbs olive oil
1 tsp ground cumin
1 tsp ground coriander
1 tbs lemon juice
1 cos (romaine) lettuce, leaves roughly torn
50 g (1 3/4 oz/1/2 punnet) snowpea (mangetout) sprouts,
  white ends trimmed

## yoghurt and caper dressing
200 g (7 oz) low-fat, thick plain yoghurt
2 tbs capers, rinsed, drained and chopped
4 tbs lemon juice

Put the chicken breasts in a shallow, non-metallic dish. In a small bowl, mix together the oil, cumin, coriander and lemon juice. Pour the mixture all over the chicken, rubbing it in thoroughly to coat all sides. Cover and leave to marinate in the fridge for 1 hour, or up to 8 hours.

Nearer to serving time, make the yoghurt and caper dressing. Put all the ingredients in a small bowl and add a few grinds of black pepper and 1–2 tablespoons of water to thin it slightly. Whisk well and set aside.

Heat a barbecue grill or chargrill pan (griddle) to medium. Add the chicken and cook for 6–8 minutes on one side, then turn and cook for a further 4 minutes, or until cooked through. Remove from the heat and leave to cool slightly, then slice into strips.

Put the lettuce and snowpea sprouts in a serving dish and add the sliced chicken. Pour over the dressing, mix gently and serve.

Serves 4

chargrilled chicken and sprout salad

## snowpea salad with japanese dressing

200 g (7 oz) snowpeas
(mangetout), tailed
50 g (1³/4 oz/¹/2 punnet)
snowpea (mangetout)
sprouts
1 small red capsicum (pepper),
julienned
2 tsp toasted sesame seeds

### japanese dressing
¹/2 tsp dashi granules
1 tbs soy sauce
1 tbs mirin
1 tsp soft brown sugar
1 garlic clove, crushed
1 tsp finely chopped fresh ginger
¹/4 tsp sesame oil
1 tbs vegetable oil
2 tsp toasted sesame seeds

Bring a pot of water to the boil, add the snowpeas and blanch for 1 minute. Drain and refresh under cold water, then drain again. Toss in a serving bowl with the snowpea sprouts and capsicum.

To make the dressing, dissolve the dashi granules in 1¹/2 tablespoons of hot water. Pour into a small bowl, add the remaining dressing ingredients and whisk well. Pour the dressing over the snowpeas, toss well and season to taste. Sprinkle with the sesame seeds and serve.

Serves 4 as a side salad

## pear and sprout salad with sesame dressing

2 small firm, ripe pears
200 g (7 oz/2 punnets) snowpea
    (mangetout) sprouts
200 g (7 oz) bean sprouts,
    tails trimmed
1 small bunch chives, snipped
    into 4 cm (1$1/2$ inch) lengths
65 g (2$1/4$ oz) snowpeas
    (mangetout), julienned
1 celery stalk, julienned

1 small handful coriander
    (cilantro) sprigs
1 tsp sesame seeds

### sesame dressing

1$1/2$ tbs soy sauce
1 tsp sesame oil
3 tsp soft brown sugar
1$1/2$ tbs peanut oil
3 tsp rice vinegar

Peel and core the pears, then slice them into thin strips. Put the pear strips in a bowl and cover with water to prevent discolouration.

Put all the sesame dressing ingredients in a small screw-top jar and shake well to dissolve the sugar.

Drain the pears and put in a large serving bowl with the snowpea sprouts, bean sprouts, chives, snowpeas, celery and coriander. Pour the dressing over, toss lightly, sprinkle with the sesame seeds and serve.

Serves 4 as a side salad

Roasting draws the sweetness from the fennel and makes a tender foil for sweet, juicy slivers of orange.

roasted fennel and orange salad

8 baby fennel bulbs
100 ml (3¹/2 fl oz) olive oil
2 oranges
1 tbs lemon juice
1 red onion, halved and thinly sliced
100 g (3¹/2 oz/¹/2 cup) Kalamata olives
2 tbs roughly chopped mint
1 tbs roughly chopped flat-leaf (Italian) parsley

Preheat the oven to 200°C (400°F/Gas 6). Trim the fronds from the fennel and reserve. Remove the stalks and cut a 5 mm (¹/4 inch) slice off the base of each fennel bulb. Slice each bulb into six wedges and arrange in a baking dish. Drizzle with 3 tablespoons of the oil and season well. Bake for 40–45 minutes, or until tender and slightly caramelized, turning once or twice during cooking. Allow to cool.

Cut a thin slice off the top and bottom of each orange. Using a sharp knife, slice off the skin and pith, removing as much of the bitter white pith as possible. Slice down the side of a segment between the flesh and the membrane (do this over a bowl to catch the juices). Repeat with the other side and lift the segment out. Remove all the segments from both oranges in the same way, squeezing out any juice remaining in the membranes.

Add the lemon juice to the juice caught from the oranges and whisk in the remaining oil until emulsified. Season well. Put the orange segments, onion and olives in a bowl, pour on half the dressing and add half the mint. Mix well, then transfer to a serving dish. Top with the fennel, drizzle with the remaining dressing and scatter with the parsley and remaining mint. Chop the reserved fennel fronds, sprinkle over the salad and serve.

Serves 4 as a side salad

snowpea salad with japanese dressing

**lunchbox** Hasty lunches snatched from the work canteen are the downfall of many a dedicated dieter, health nut or office gourmand, and yet organizing a packed lunch can seem all too daunting in

the cold light of morning. Not anymore. Here's all the inspiration you need to plan ahead a little and pack a pretty lunchbox with a super energy-giving salad to power you through the day.

Being aware of what we eat is not just about watching our weight. For many of us it is simply about aspiring to an optimal state of health and wellbeing. Evaluating the quality of the food we consume is a simple way to stay on top and, by and large, most of us manage to do pretty well, except for the daily downfall — lunch on the run. If you're in the habit of buying lunch, whether from a food court, deli, canteen or fast-food joint, it can be hard to know what you are really consuming. And while schooldays may have ruined your appetite for packed lunches, it's time to relinquish those musty memories of soggy sandwiches and browning bananas. Variety, sustenance and balance are easy to achieve on a daily basis when you explore the range of delicious salads that are perfect for packing up and taking with you. It's so simple to create inspiring and healthy lunches: all the recipes in this chapter can be made ahead and packed the night before, ready to pop in your bag as you're dashing out the door. Even better, there's enough for two helpings, so pack another lunchbox for a loved one, or save it for the following day. And when it comes to stashing your salad, you can always resort to the ever-sensible plastic lunchbox, or you could really have some fun and break up the humdrum routine. Noodle boxes, kitsch creations and tiffin stacks are just a couple of ideas to dress it all up. Takeaway chopsticks and funky napkins are a cute way to treat yourself as you would someone else — like you are special and deserve the extra treatment. Now there's something to look forward to in the middle of the workaday day!

## asian tofu salad

¹/2 red capsicum (pepper)
¹/2 green capsicum (pepper)
60 g (2¹/4 oz/²/3 cup) bean
   sprouts, tails trimmed
2 spring onions (scallions), sliced
1 tbs chopped coriander (cilantro)
200 g (7 oz/3 cups) shredded
   Chinese cabbage
1¹/2 tbs chopped roasted peanuts
200 g (7 oz) firm tofu
1¹/2 tbs peanut oil

**dressing**
1 tbs sweet chilli sauce
1 tbs lime juice
¹/4 tsp sesame oil
3 tsp light soy sauce
1 garlic clove, finely chopped
1¹/2 tsp finely grated fresh
   ginger
1¹/2 tbs peanut oil

Thinly slice the red and green capsicum and toss in a large bowl with the bean sprouts, spring onion, coriander, cabbage and peanuts.

Cut the tofu into 8 cm x 2 cm (3¹/4 x ³/4 inch) steaks. Heat the oil in a large frying pan and cook the tofu over medium heat for 2–3 minutes on each side, or until golden with a crispy edge. Add the tofu to the salad.

To make the dressing, whisk all the ingredients in a small bowl until well combined. Toss through the salad and divide between two lunchboxes.

Makes 2 lunchbox salads

## asian pork salad

### ginger and chilli dressing
3 cm (1$^{1}/_{4}$ inch) piece of fresh
    ginger, peeled and julienned
1 tsp rice vinegar
$^{1}/_{2}$ small red chilli, seeded
    and finely chopped
1 tbs light soy sauce
a few drops of sesame oil
$^{1}/_{2}$ star anise
1 tsp lime juice

125 g (4$^{1}/_{2}$ oz) Chinese roast
    pork (char siu)
50 g (1$^{3}/_{4}$ oz/$^{1}/_{2}$ punnet)
    snowpea (mangetout)
    sprouts
2 spring onions (scallions), thinly
    sliced on the diagonal
$^{1}/_{2}$ small red capsicum (pepper),
    thinly sliced

To make the ginger and chilli dressing, combine the ginger, vinegar, chilli, soy sauce, sesame oil, star anise and lime juice in a small saucepan. Gently warm for 2 minutes, or until just about to come to the boil, then set aside to cool. Once it has cooled, remove the star anise.

Thinly slice the pork and divide among two lunchboxes along with the snowpea sprouts, spring onion and capsicum. Pack the dressing separately and drizzle over the salad just before eating.

Makes 2 lunchbox salads

Wild rice has a tough shell but a tender heart. Its nutty flavour brings a satisfying bite to this surprisingly feisty salad.

### chinese barbecue roast chicken with wild rice

50 g (1¾ oz/¼ cup) wild rice
50 g (1¾ oz/¼ cup) jasmine
   rice
½ small Chinese barbecue
   roast chicken
3 tsp chopped mint
3 tsp chopped coriander
   (cilantro)
½ Lebanese (short) cucumber
2 spring onions (scallions),
   sliced on the diagonal

3 tsp roasted unsalted peanuts,
   roughly chopped
sweet chilli sauce, to serve

mirin dressing
2 tsp mirin
1 tsp Chinese rice wine
½ tsp soy sauce
½ tsp lime juice
1 tsp sweet chilli sauce

Bring a large pot of water to the boil and add the wild rice and 1 teaspoon of salt. Cook for 30 minutes, then add the jasmine rice and cook for a further 10 minutes, or until both rices are tender. Drain the rice, refresh under cold water and drain again.

Shred the chicken (including the skin) into bite-sized pieces and put in a large bowl. Add the mint and coriander. Cut the cucumber through the centre (do not peel) and thinly slice it on the diagonal. Add to the chicken with the rice, spring onion and peanuts.

Mix together all the mirin dressing ingredients in a small jug, pour over the salad and toss to combine. Divide between two lunchboxes and drizzle with a little sweet chilli sauce.

Makes 2 lunchbox salads

asian pork salad

## farfalle salad with sun-dried tomatoes and spinach

165 g (5³/4 oz) farfalle or
   spiral pasta
1 spring onion (scallion), finely
   sliced on the diagonal
3 sun-dried tomatoes, cut
   into strips
350 g (12 oz) English spinach,
   stalks trimmed and leaves
   shredded

1 tbs toasted pine nuts
1 tsp chopped oregano

dressing
1 tbs olive oil
1/4 tsp chopped chilli
1 small garlic clove, crushed

Cook the pasta in a large pot of rapidly boiling salted water until al dente. Drain, rinse under cold water and drain again. Allow the pasta to cool, then transfer to a large bowl. Add the spring onion, tomato, spinach, pine nuts and oregano.

Put all the dressing ingredients in a small screw-top jar and season with salt and pepper. Shake well and pour all over the salad. Gently toss together and divide between two lunchboxes.

Makes 2 lunchbox salads

## haloumi and asparagus salad with salsa verde

**salsa verde**
1 small handful basil leaves
1 small handful mint leaves
1 large handful parsley leaves
1 tbs baby capers, rinsed
   and drained
1 garlic clove
1 tbs olive oil

1/2 tbs lemon juice
1/2 tbs lime juice

125 g (41/2 oz) haloumi cheese
175 g (6 oz/1 bunch) thin
   asparagus spears
1 tbs garlic oil or olive oil
50 g (13/4 oz) mixed salad leaves

To make the salsa verde, blend the herbs, capers, garlic and oil in a food processor until smooth. Add the lemon and lime juice, and pulse briefly.

Heat a chargrill pan (griddle) to medium. Cut the haloumi into 1 cm (1/2 inch) slices, then cut each slice into two small triangles. Brush the haloumi and asparagus with the garlic oil. Chargrill the asparagus for 1 minute or until just tender, then chargrill the haloumi for about 45 seconds on each side, or until grill marks appear.

Divide the salad leaves between two lunchboxes and top with the haloumi and asparagus. Pack the salsa verde separately and drizzle over the salad just before eating.

Makes 2 lunchbox salads

Crispy apple, bitey radish, peppery rocket and smoky chicken:
this snappy salad will pick you up in a flash.

## smoked chicken and pasta salad with mustard dressing

100 g (3½ oz) bucatini pasta
  (see Note)
250 g (9 oz) good-quality
  smoked chicken breast
1 small Fuji apple
4 small radishes, thinly sliced
2 spring onions (scallions),
  finely sliced

50 g (1⅓ oz/½ small bunch)
  rocket (arugula), trimmed

**mustard dressing**
½ tbs balsamic vinegar
3½ tbs olive oil
½ tbs lemon juice
1½ tbs wholegrain mustard

Cook the pasta in a large pot of rapidly boiling salted water until al dente.
Drain, rinse under cold water and drain again. Place in a large bowl.

Put all the mustard dressing ingredients in a screw-top jar and shake well. Season to taste with salt and freshly cracked pepper. Toss one-third of the dressing through the pasta and set aside for 30 minutes.

Cut the chicken breast into strips on the diagonal and place in a bowl. Leaving the skin on the apple, cut it into quarters, then core the quarters and cut them into cubes. Add them to the chicken with the radish, spring onion and rocket. Pour over the remaining dressing and toss lightly.

Gently toss the chicken mixture through the pasta until well combined. Divide between two lunchboxes and enjoy with fresh, crusty bread.

Note: Bucatini is a thick, spaghetti-like pasta with a hollow centre and a chewy texture.

Makes 2 lunchbox salads

haloumi and asparagus salad with salsa verde

## avocado, bacon and tomato salad

3 garlic cloves, unpeeled
2 tbs olive oil
3 tsp balsamic vinegar
1 tsp Dijon mustard
125 g (4½ oz) rindless smoked
   back bacon (see Note) or
   middle bacon rashers

50 g (1¾ oz) green salad leaves
½ small red onion, finely sliced
1 avocado, cut into chunks
2 small firm, ripe tomatoes,
   cut into chunks

Preheat the oven to 180°C (350°F/Gas 4). Place the unpeeled garlic cloves on a baking tray and roast for 30 minutes. Remove, allow to cool, then squeeze the flesh out of the skins and mash in a small bowl. Add the oil, vinegar and mustard, whisk well to make a dressing and season to taste.

Chop the bacon into bite-sized pieces, then cook under a medium-hot grill (broiler) or dry-fry in a frying pan over medium heat for 3–5 minutes, or until crisp. Divide between two lunchboxes with the salad leaves, onion, avocado and tomato. Gently toss together. Pack the dressing separately and, just before eating, give it a good shake and drizzle over the salad.

Note: Smoked back bacon is available from most delicatessens. If you can't obtain any, you can use bacon rashers instead.

Makes 2 lunchbox salads

# chilli chicken and cashew salad

2 tsp olive oil
300 g (10$^1$/$_2$ oz) chicken breast
   fillets
50 g (1$^3$/$_4$ oz) salad leaves
125 g (4$^1$/$_2$ oz/$^1$/$_2$ punnet) cherry
   tomatoes, halved
$^1$/$_2$ Lebanese (short) cucumber,
   cut into bite-sized chunks
50 g (1$^3$/$_4$ oz/$^1$/$_2$ punnet) snowpea
   (mangetout) sprouts, trimmed
40 g (1$^1$/$_2$ oz/$^1$/$_4$ cup) cashew
   nuts, roughly chopped

dressing
1$^1$/$_2$ tbs sweet chilli sauce
1 tbs lime juice
1 tsp fish sauce
1 tbs chopped coriander
   (cilantro)
1 small garlic clove, crushed
$^1$/$_2$ small red chilli, finely
   chopped
1 teaspoon grated fresh ginger
2 tsp peanut or sesame oil

Heat the oil in a frying pan or chargrill pan (griddle). Add the chicken and cook over medium heat for 5–8 minutes on each side, or until cooked through. While still hot, slice each breast widthways into strips.

Combine the dressing ingredients in a large bowl and mix well. Toss the warm chicken strips through the dressing and leave to cool slightly. Divide the salad leaves, tomato, cucumber and snowpea sprouts between two lunchboxes and scatter with the cashews. Pack the dressed chicken separately and mix through the salad just before eating.

Makes 2 lunchbox salads

Marinating chicken makes it exquisitely tender, and allows all the dusky, musky spices to permeate deep into the meat.

## indian marinated chicken salad

1¹/2 tbs lemon juice
1 teaspoon garam masala
¹/2 tsp ground turmeric
2 tsp finely grated fresh ginger
1 garlic clove, finely chopped
1¹/2 tbs vegetable oil
325 g (11¹/2 oz) chicken breast
    fillets
¹/2 onion, thinly sliced
1 zucchini (courgette), thinly
    sliced on the diagonal
60 g (2¹/4 oz/2 cups) picked
    watercress leaves

80 g (2³/4 oz/¹/2 cup) freshly
    podded peas
1 tomato, finely chopped
1 small handful coriander
    (cilantro) leaves

yoghurt dressing
¹/2 tsp cumin seeds
¹/4 tsp coriander seeds
2 tbs thick plain yoghurt
1 tbs chopped mint
1 tbs lemon juice

Combine the lemon juice, garam masala, turmeric, ginger, garlic and 1 teaspoon of the oil in a large bowl. Add the chicken and onion, toss well to coat all over, then cover and refrigerate for 1 hour.

Remove the onion from the chicken marinade, then heat 1 tablespoon of the oil in a large frying pan. Cook the chicken over medium heat for about 4–5 minutes on each side, or until cooked through. Remove the chicken from the pan and leave to rest for 5 minutes. Cut each breast across the grain into 1 cm (1/2 inch) slices.

Heat the remaining oil in the pan and sauté the zucchini and marinated onion for 2 minutes, or until lightly golden and tender. Toss in a large bowl with the watercress. Cook the peas in boiling water for 5 minutes, or until tender, then drain and rinse under cold water to cool. Add to the salad with the chicken, tomato and coriander.

To make the yoghurt dressing, dry-fry the cumin and coriander seeds in a frying pan over medium heat for 1–2 minutes, or until fragrant. Put the seeds in a mortar and pestle (or spice grinder) and pound them to a powder. Mix together with the yoghurt, mint and lemon juice. Gently fold the dressing through the salad and divide between two lunchboxes.

Makes 2 lunchbox salads

chilli chicken and
cashew salad

## tomato and bocconcini salad

basil oil
125 ml (4 fl oz/½ cup) olive oil
1 large handful basil leaves,
   torn
1 tbs balsamic vinegar

3 Roma (plum) tomatoes, halved
175 g (6 oz) cherry bocconcini
   or baby mozzarella cheese
80 g (2¾ oz) mizuna lettuce
   leaves or baby rocket
   (arugula) leaves

To make the basil oil, put the oil and basil leaves in a saucepan. Stir gently over medium heat for 3–5 minutes, or until very hot but not smoking. Remove from the heat and discard the basil. Reserve 1 tablespoon of the basil oil and mix it with the vinegar; store the remaining basil oil in a clean jar in the refrigerator to use in salad dressings and pasta sauces.

Arrange the tomato, bocconcini and lettuce in two lunchboxes. Drizzle with the basil oil and sprinkle with sea salt and cracked black pepper.

Makes 2 lunchbox salads

## caramelized onion and potato salad

1 tbs olive oil
3 red onions, thinly sliced
500 g (1 lb 2 oz) kipfler or new
    potatoes, unpeeled
2 rashers of streaky bacon,
    rind removed
1/2 bunch chives, snipped

lemon mayonnaise
125 g (4$^{1}$/$_{2}$ oz/ $^{1}$/$_{2}$ cup)
    ready-made whole-egg
    mayonnaise
2 tsp Dijon mustard
1/2 lemon, juiced
1 tbs sour cream

Heat the oil in a large heavy-based frying pan. Add the onion and cook, stirring, over low heat for 40 minutes, or until soft and caramelized.

Cut any large potatoes into large chunks (leave the small ones whole). Cook in boiling water for 10 minutes, or until just tender, then drain. Place in a large bowl with the onion and most of the chives and mix well.

Meanwhile, grill (broil) the bacon rashers until crisp. Drain on crumpled paper towels and allow to cool slightly, then chop coarsely.

Whisk together the lemon mayonnaise ingredients, pour over the salad and toss to coat. Divide between two lunchboxes and sprinkle with the bacon and reserved chives.

Makes 2 lunchbox salads

The classic clash of sweet and sour is a delectable match for tender pork, jazzed up with sweet pineapple and crunchy nuts.

## sweet and sour pork salad

marinade
1 tbs soy sauce
2 tsp runny honey
2 tsp dry sherry

250 g (9 oz) pork fillet, trimmed
1 tbs peanut oil
100 g (3¹/₂ oz) Chinese cabbage, finely shredded

1 small carrot, grated
2 spring onions (scallions), finely sliced on the diagonal
300 g (10 oz) tin pineapple pieces, drained (reserve 1 tbs of the juice)
1 tbs white wine vinegar
¹/₄ tsp soft brown sugar

Put all the marinade ingredients in a small screw-top jar and shake well.

Place the pork fillet in a bowl and pour over the marinade. Turn to coat all sides, then cover with plastic wrap and refrigerate for at least 2 hours — or preferably overnight — turning occasionally.

Heat half the oil in a heavy-based pan. Add the pork fillet and cook over medium heat for 10 minutes, turning to brown all sides. Remove to a plate and cover loosely with foil. Leave to cool, then slice.

Toss the cabbage, carrot, spring onion and pineapple together in a large bowl. Put the reserved pineapple juice in a small screw-top jar with the remaining oil, vinegar and sugar and shake well. Pour the dressing over the salad and toss gently to combine. Divide between two lunchboxes and top with the sliced pork.

Makes 2 lunchbox salads

tomato and bocconcini salad

## tuscan bread salad

3 thick slices of an Italian-style
    bread such as ciabatta,
    crusts removed
2 large vine-ripened tomatoes
1½ tbs olive oil
1 tsp lemon juice

2 tsp red wine vinegar
2 anchovy fillets, finely chopped
1 teaspoon baby capers, rinsed,
    drained and finely chopped
1 garlic clove, crushed
1 handful basil leaves

Preheat the oven to 220°C (425°F/Gas 7). Tear the bread into 2 cm (3/4 inch) chunks, then spread on a baking tray and bake for 5–7 minutes, or until golden. Leave on a cake rack to cool.

Score a cross in the base of each tomato. Place in a heatproof bowl and cover with boiling water. Leave for 30 seconds, then plunge in cold water and peel the skin from the cross. Cut a tomato in half and squeeze the juice and seeds into a bowl; chop and reserve the flesh. Add the oil, lemon juice, vinegar, anchovies, capers and garlic to the tomato juice, and season.

Seed and slice the remaining tomato, and place in a large bowl with the reserved chopped tomato flesh and most of the basil. Add the dressing and toasted bread and toss. Divide between two lunchboxes, scatter with the remaining basil, then season. Serve at room temperature.

Makes 2 lunchbox salads

## herbed feta salad

1 small slice thick white bread,
    crust removed
75 g (2$^1$/$_2$ oz) feta cheese, cut
    into cubes
$^1$/$_4$ red coral lettuce, leaves torn
$^1$/$_4$ butter, coral or oakleaf
    lettuce, leaves torn

dressing
1 small garlic clove, crushed
1 heaped tsp finely chopped
    marjoram
1 heaped tsp finely snipped
    chives
1 heaped tsp finely chopped basil
3 tsp white wine vinegar
1$^1$/$_2$ tbs olive oil

Preheat the oven to 180°C (350°F/Gas 4). Cut the bread into cubes and spread on a baking tray. Bake for 10 minutes, or until crisp and lightly golden. Put the tray on a rack and leave to cool completely.

Put the feta in a bowl. Combine all the dressing ingredients in a small screw-top jar and shake for 30 seconds. Pour over the feta, cover with plastic wrap and leave to marinate in the refrigerator, stirring occasionally.

Divide the lettuce leaves and bread cubes between two lunchboxes. Pack the dressed feta separately and mix it through the salad just before eating.

Makes 2 lunchbox salads

There's no nicer way to use up leftover chicken than this tasty salad studded with plump sultanas and creamy cashews.

## chicken with mixed rice, sultanas and toasted cashews

135 g (5 oz/2/3 cup) mixed rice blend (see Note)
50 g (13/4 oz/1/3 cup) cashew nuts
100 g (31/2 oz) shredded roast or barbecued chicken
40 g (11/2 oz/1/3 cup) sultanas
8–10 coriander (cilantro) sprigs

coriander dressing
2 tbs olive oil
1 tbs red wine vinegar
1 tsp seeded mustard
2 tbs finely chopped coriander (cilantro) leaves

Cook the rice according to the packet instructions, then drain well. Rinse under cold water and drain well again. Fluff up with a fork to separate the grains, then leave to cool in a sieve over a saucepan.

While the rice is cooling, put a frying pan over high heat. Add the cashews and dry-fry for 1–2 minutes, tossing them about so they colour evenly. When the nuts are lightly toasted, put them on a chopping board, leave to cool, then roughly chop them.

Put all the coriander dressing ingredients except the coriander leaves in a small bowl and whisk until well combined. Season lightly with salt and black pepper, then stir in the coriander.

When the rice is cold, mix through the shredded chicken, cashews and sultanas. Stir in the dressing, season with salt and pepper and mix well. Divide between two lunchboxes and scatter with coriander sprigs.

Note: You could also use leftover rice for this recipe. You will need about 350 g (12 oz/2 cups) of cold cooked rice.

Makes 2 lunchbox salads

chicken with mixed rice, sultanas and toasted cashews

## minty lentil salad

90 g (3¹/₄ oz/¹/₂ cup) brown
    lentils
¹/₂ chicken or vegetable stock
    cube, crumbled
1 tomato, cut into 1 cm
    (¹/₂ inch) cubes
2 spring onions (scallions), sliced

**mint dressing**
1 tbs oil
1 tsp apple cider vinegar
2 tsp chopped mint
¹/₄ tsp ground cumin
pinch of cayenne pepper

Put the lentils in a pot, cover with cold water and add the stock cube. Bring to the boil, then reduce the heat and simmer for 20 minutes, or until the lentils are tender — don't overcook or the lentils will become mushy. Drain and set aside to cool.

Gently toss the lentils in a bowl with the tomato and spring onion. Put the mint dressing ingredients in a small screw-top jar and shake well. Drizzle the dressing over the salad, toss gently to combine, then divide between two lunchboxes. Delicious with fresh, crusty bread.

Makes 2 lunchbox salads

## beetroot and chive salad

12 baby beetroot
2 tablespoons pine nuts or
    pistachio nuts
30 g (1 oz/1 cup) picked
    watercress leaves
1 tbs snipped chives

**dressing**
$1/4$ tsp honey
$1/4$ tsp Dijon mustard
3 tsp balsamic vinegar
$1^{1}/_{2}$ tbs olive oil

Preheat the oven to 200°C (400°F/Gas 6). Trim the beetroot bulbs and scrub them well. Put them in a roasting dish, cover with foil and roast for 1 hour, or until tender. Remove from the oven and leave to cool.

Turn the oven down to 180°C (350°F/Gas 4). Spread the nuts on a baking tray and bake for 5 minutes, or until lightly golden, ensuring they don't burn. Remove from the oven, leave to cool, then roughly chop.

To make the dressing, combine the honey, mustard and vinegar in a small jug. Whisk in the oil with a fork until well combined, then season to taste.

Peel the beetroot, wearing gloves, and halve any larger ones. Divide between two lunchboxes with the watercress and chives, and scatter with the nuts. Pack the dressing separately and drizzle over the salad just before eating.

Makes 2 lunchbox salads

Beetroots burst with sweet, mellow flavour, and here their scarlet juices mingle with creamy white goat's cheese.

## fresh beetroot and goat's cheese salad

2 beetroot bulbs, with leaves
100 g (3½ oz) green beans, trimmed
50 g (1¾ oz) goat's cheese

caper dressing
2 tsp red wine vinegar
1 tbs extra virgin olive oil
1 garlic clove, crushed
2 tsp capers, rinsed, drained and coarsely chopped

Trim the leaves from the beetroot. Scrub the bulbs and wash the leaves well. Bring a large pot of water to the boil, add the beetroot, then reduce the heat and simmer, covered, for about 30 minutes, or until tender. Drain and allow to cool. Wearing gloves to protect your hands from staining, peel the skins off the beetroot and cut the bulbs into wedges.

Meanwhile, bring a pot of lightly salted water to the boil, add the beans and blanch until bright green and just tender, about 2–3 minutes. Remove with tongs and plunge into a bowl of cold water. Drain well.

Add the beetroot leaves to the pot of boiling water and cook for about 3–5 minutes, or until the leaves and stems are tender. Drain, plunge into a bowl of cold water, then drain well again.

To make the caper dressing, put the vinegar, oil, garlic and capers in a small screw-top jar with 1/4 teaspoon each of salt and cracked black pepper. Shake vigorously until well combined.

Divide the beans, beetroot and beetroot leaves between two lunchboxes. Crumble the goat's cheese over the top and drizzle with the dressing.

Makes 2 lunchbox salads

beetroot and chive salad

## egg salad with dill mayonnaise

**dill mayonnaise**
1 egg yolk
3 tsp lemon juice
2 tsp Dijon mustard
70 ml (2¼ fl oz) olive oil
70 ml (2¼ fl oz) safflower oil
2 tbs chopped dill

30 g (1 oz) crème fraîche or
    sour cream
2 tbs baby capers, rinsed and
    drained

5 large hard-boiled eggs, peeled
20 g (¾ oz) mustard cress

To make the dill mayonnaise, put the egg yolk, lemon juice and mustard in a food processor or blender and season with salt and pepper. With the motor running, slowly add the combined olive oil and safflower oil, drop by drop at first, then slowly increasing the amount to a thin, steady stream as the mixture thickens. When all the oil has been added, put the mayonnaise in a bowl and gently stir in the dill, crème fraîche and capers. This mayonnaise makes enough for more than one use, so transfer half the mayonnaise to a clean container and refrigerate for use in another salad.

Roughly chop the eggs and fold into the remaining mayonnaise, then divide between two lunchboxes. Cut the green tips from the mustard cress and scatter them over the salad. Delicious with fresh, crusty bread.

Makes 2 lunchbox salads

# chargrilled vegetable salad with balsamic dressing

2 baby eggplants (aubergines)
2 large Roma (plum) tomatoes
1 red capsicum (pepper)
1/2 green capsicum (pepper)
1 zucchini (courgette)
2 1/2 tbs olive oil
6 bocconcini or 12 small, fresh
    mozzarella cheeses

12 Ligurian olives
1 garlic clove, finely chopped
1 heaped tsp baby capers,
    rinsed and drained
1/4 tsp sugar
1 tbs balsamic vinegar

Cut the eggplants and tomatoes into quarters. Cut the capsicums in half lengthways, remove the seeds and membrane, then cut each half into thick strips. Thinly slice the zucchini on the diagonal.

Preheat a chargrill pan (griddle) or barbecue hotplate to high. Brush with 1/2 tablespoon of the oil and cook the vegetables in batches for about 2–3 minutes, or until golden and slightly charred, adding a little more oil as needed. (The tomatoes are best cooked cut-side-down first.)

Put the vegetables and cheese in a large bowl. Mix together the olives, garlic, capers, sugar and vinegar with the remaining oil, then pour over the salad and toss. Divide between two lunchboxes and sprinkle with pepper.

Makes 2 lunchbox salads

Fresh and wholesome, this cool, crunchy salad has a wicked streak — a sprinkling of incredibly addictive garlic croutons.

## snowpea salad

garlic croutons
1 1/2 slices thick white bread, crusts removed
3 tbs olive oil
1 small garlic clove, crushed

dressing
1 tbs olive oil
2 tsp mayonnaise
2 tsp sour cream
1 tbs lemon juice
1/2 tsp soft brown sugar

100 g (3 1/2 oz) snowpeas (mangetout), tailed and sliced diagonally
1/2 red capsicum (pepper), sliced
125 g (4 oz/1/2 punnet) cherry tomatoes
30 g (1 oz/1 cup) picked watercress sprigs
2 oakleaf lettuce leaves, torn
2 green coral lettuce leaves, torn
shaved Parmesan cheese, to serve

To make the garlic croutons, cut the bread into 1 cm ($^1/_2$ inch) cubes. Heat the oil in a small, heavy-based frying pan and add the garlic. Stir in the bread cubes and cook over medium heat for about 4–5 minutes, or until golden and crisp. Remove from the pan and leave to drain thoroughly on crumpled paper towels.

Whisk all the dressing ingredients in a small bowl with some cracked black pepper for 2 minutes, or until well combined.

Divide the snowpeas, capsicum, tomato, watercress and lettuce leaves between two lunchboxes. Scatter some Parmesan over the top. Pack the croutons in a separate container so they stay crisp, and take the dressing in a separate container so the lettuce doesn't go soggy. Just before eating, drizzle the dressing over the salad and scatter with the croutons.

Makes 2 lunchbox salads

chargrilled vegetable salad with
balsamic dressing

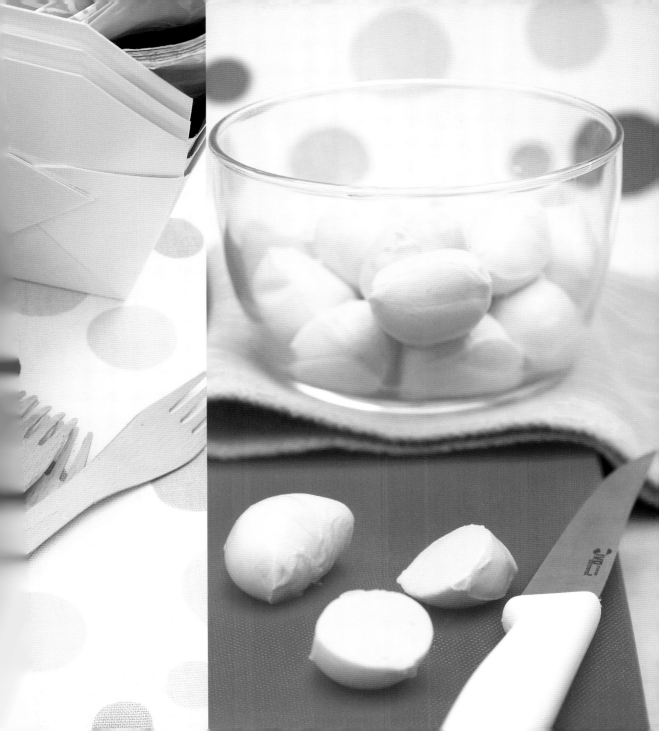

## vietnamese salad with lemon grass dressing

100 g (3½ oz) dried rice
    vermicelli
1 small handful Vietnamese
    mint leaves, torn
1 small handful coriander
    (cilantro) leaves
½ small red onion, thinly sliced
1 small green mango, peeled
    and julienned
½ Lebanese (short) cucumber,
    halved and thinly sliced
80 g (2¾ oz/½ cup) crushed
    peanuts

**lemon grass dressing**
3 tbs lime juice
2 tsp grated palm sugar or
    soft brown sugar
1½ tbs seasoned rice vinegar
1 stem lemon grass, white part
    only, finely chopped
1 red chilli, seeded and finely
    chopped
1 makrut (kaffir lime) leaf,
    shredded

Put the noodles in a bowl, cover with boiling water and soak for 10 minutes, or until soft. Drain, rinse under cold water and cut into short lengths. Toss in a large bowl with the mint, coriander, onion, mango, cucumber and three-quarters of the nuts, then divide between two lunchboxes.

Whisk the dressing ingredients together and toss through the salad. Pack the remaining nuts separately and sprinkle over the salad just before eating.

Makes 2 lunchbox salads

## cottage cheese salad

1/2 sheet lavash bread
1 tsp canola oil
pinch of mild paprika
1 tbs snipped chives
250 g (9 oz) cottage cheese

8 red oakleaf lettuce leaves
100 g (31/2 oz) red grapes
1 small carrot, grated
2 tbs alfalfa sprouts

Preheat the oven to 180°C (350°F/Gas 4). Brush the lavash with the oil, sprinkle lightly with paprika and cut into eight strips. Spread on a baking tray and bake for 5 minutes, or until golden. Leave to cool on a rack.

Mix the chives through the cottage cheese. Divide the lettuce, grapes and carrot between two lunchboxes, then arrange the cottage cheese and sprouts on top. Pack the lavash crisps separately so they don't become soggy, and eat them with the salad.

Makes 2 lunchbox salads

Tender vegetables smothered in an irresistible satay dressing: this Indonesian classic will send your tastebuds spinning!

## gado gado

1 small carrot, thinly sliced
50 g (3/4 oz/1/2 cup) small
    cauliflower florets
6–8 snowpeas (mangetout),
    tailed
50 g (3/4 oz/heaped 1/2 cup)
    bean sprouts, tails trimmed
4 well-shaped iceberg lettuce
    leaves
2 small potatoes, cooked and
    cut into thin slices
1/2 Lebanese (short) cucumber,
    thinly sliced

1 hard-boiled egg, peeled and
    cut into quarters
1 tomato, cut into wedges

peanut sauce
2 tsp oil
1/2 small onion, finely chopped
3 tbs crunchy peanut butter
90 ml (3 fl oz) coconut milk
1/2 tsp sambal oelek
2 tsp lemon juice
2 tsp kecap manis

Steam the carrot and cauliflower in a pot of boiling water for 5 minutes, or until nearly tender. Add the snowpeas and cook for 2 minutes. Add the bean sprouts and cook for 1 minute more, then set aside and allow to cool.

To make the peanut sauce, heat the oil in a saucepan and sauté the onion for 5 minutes over low heat, or until soft and lightly golden. Add the peanut butter, coconut milk, sambal oelek, lemon juice, kecap manis and 3 tablespoons water, and stir well. Bring to the boil, stirring constantly, then reduce the heat and simmer for 5 minutes, or until the sauce has reduced and thickened. Remove from the heat.

Sit one lettuce leaf inside another to form a lettuce cup. Make another lettuce cup in the same way and put them in two lunchboxes. Arrange half the potato, carrot, cauliflower, snowpeas, bean sprouts and cucumber in each lettuce cup, then top with the egg and tomato. Pack the peanut sauce separately and drizzle over the salad just before eating.

Makes 2 lunchbox salads

vietnamese salad with lemon grass dressing

## burghul, feta and parsley salad

90 g (3¼ oz/½ cup) burghul
   (bulgar) wheat
2 tbs chopped flat-leaf (Italian)
   parsley
2 tbs chopped mint
4 spring onions (scallions),
   finely chopped

2 firm ripe tomatoes, halved,
   seeded and diced
1 short (Lebanese) cucumber,
   halved, seeded and diced
100 g (3½ oz) feta, crumbled
2 tbs lemon juice
2 tbs olive oil

Put the burghul in a large bowl and add enough hot water to cover. Leave to soak for 15–20 minutes, or until tender. Drain well, then thoroughly squeeze out all the excess liquid.

Gently toss the burghul in a bowl with all the remaining ingredients. Season with sea salt and freshly ground black pepper and mix together well. Divide between two lunchboxes and leave for at least an hour to allow all the flavours to mingle.

Makes 2 lunchbox salads

# frisée salad with speck and croutons

vinaigrette
1/2 French shallot (eschalot),
   finely chopped
2 tsp Dijon mustard
1 1/2 tbs tarragon vinegar
4 tbs extra virgin olive oil

2 tsp olive oil
125 g (4 1/2 oz) speck, rind
   removed, cut into fine strips
1/4 baguette, sliced
2 garlic cloves
1/2 baby frisée (curly endive),
   washed and dried
50 g (3/4 oz/1/2 cup) toasted
   walnuts

To make the vinaigrette, whisk the shallot, mustard and vinegar in a small bowl. Slowly add the oil, whisking constantly until thickened. Set aside.

Heat the olive oil in a large frying pan. Add the speck, bread slices and whole garlic cloves and cook over medium heat for 5–8 minutes, or until the bread and speck are both crisp. Discard the garlic.

Arrange the speck in two lunchboxes with the frisée and walnuts. Pack the toasted bread slices separately so they stay crisp, and carry the vinaigrette separately so the lettuce doesn't become soggy. Just before eating, drizzle the vinaigrette over the salad and scatter with the croutons.

Makes 2 lunchbox salads

Couscous is the ultimate flavour absorber, soaking up the
aromatic dressing and making a fluffy base for nuts and vegies.

## couscous salad

40 g (1¼ oz/¼ cup) shelled
    pistachio nuts
175 g (6 oz) peeled jap
    pumpkin, thinly sliced
1 zucchini (courgette), sliced
1½ tbs olive oil
½ red capsicum (pepper)
185 g (6½ oz/1 cup) instant
    couscous
300 g (10½ oz) tin chickpeas,
    drained and rinsed
2 spring onions (scallions), sliced
1 handful mint, shredded

dressing
1 tsp cumin seeds
1 garlic clove, finely chopped
1 small red chilli, seeded and
    finely chopped
125 ml (4 fl oz/½ cup) chicken
    or vegetable stock
2 fresh bay leaves, torn
2 tbs lemon juice
3 tbs extra virgin olive oil

Preheat the oven to 180°C (350°F/Gas 4). Spread the pistachios on a baking
tray and bake for 5–10 minutes, or until lightly golden — keep an eye on
them as they burn easily. Remove, leave to cool, then roughly chop.

Drizzle the pumpkin and zucchini with 1 tablespoon of the oil. Cook under a hot grill (broiler) for 4–5 minutes on each side, or until golden.

Cut the capsicum into large flat pieces and remove the seeds and membranes. Cook, skin-side-up, under the hot grill (broiler) until the skin blackens and blisters. Leave to cool in a plastic bag, then peel away the skin and cut the flesh into 1 cm (1/2 inch) strips.

Put the couscous in a large bowl. Cover with 250 ml (9 fl oz/1 cup) boiling water, add the remaining oil and stir gently. Cover with plastic wrap and leave for 5 minutes. Fluff up the couscous with a fork, raking out any lumps, then add the pistachios, pumpkin, zucchini, capsicum, chickpeas, spring onion and mint. Toss well.

To make the dressing, gently dry-fry the cumin seeds in a heavy-based frying pan for 1–2 minutes, or until fragrant. Pound to a powder in a mortar and pestle, then place in a bowl and mix in the garlic and chilli.

Boil the stock in a saucepan with the bay leaves for 2 minutes, or until reduced to 2 tablespoons of liquid. Strain the stock into the spice mixture and discard the bay leaves. Add the lemon juice, then whisk in the oil with a fork. Season to taste, then gently toss through the couscous and divide between two lunchboxes.

Makes 2 lunchbox salads

burghul, feta and parsley salad

## crunchy rice salad

100 g (3 1/2 oz/1/2 cup) basmati
   or jasmine rice
1 carrot, sliced diagonally
1/2 green capsicum (pepper),
   julienned
100 g (3 1/2 oz) baby corn, cut
   into 2 cm (3/4 inch) lengths
1 spring onion (scallion), sliced

75 g (2 1/2 oz) Chinese roast pork
   (char siu), thinly sliced

**dressing**
1 tbs peanut oil
2 tsp sesame oil
1 tsp lime juice
1 tsp soy sauce

Cook the rice in a large pot of boiling water until just tender. Drain, rinse under cold water and drain again thoroughly. Spread over a plate and leave to cool. When the rice has cooled, toss it in a bowl with the carrot, capsicum, corn, spring onion and pork.

Put the dressing ingredients in a small screw-top jar and shake well. Pour over the salad and toss well, then divide between two lunchboxes.

Makes 2 lunchbox salads

## roasted beet salad

3 beetroot bulbs, with leaves
6 French shallots (eschalots),
    unpeeled
6 garlic cloves, unpeeled
2 tsp vegetable oil
1 handful baby beetroot leaves
25 g (1 oz/¹/₄ cup) toasted walnuts

**dressing**
1 tbs red wine vinegar
2 tbs walnut oil
1 small garlic clove, crushed
¹/₂ tsp Dijon mustard

Preheat the oven to 200°C (400°F/Gas 6). Cut the leaves off the beetroot, wash well and reserve. Scrub the bulbs, place in a roasting tin with the shallots and garlic cloves and roast for 1 hour. Remove the shallots and garlic and roast the beetroot for another 30 minutes, or until tender.

Whisk the dressing ingredients in a small bowl, then season well with sea salt and pepper. Slip the shallots and garlic from their skins into a large bowl. Peel the beetroot bulbs, cut them into wedges and add them to the shallots. Gently mix the dressing through, then cool to room temperature.

Divide the beetroot mixture between two lunchboxes and season well with sea salt and pepper. Pack the beetroot leaves and walnuts separately and mix them through the salad just before eating.

Makes 2 lunchbox salads

Orange zest and basil add a lively counterpoint to the deep, mellow flavours of roasted vegetables and nutty brown rice.

brown rice, tuna and roasted vegetable salad

1 small red capsicum (pepper), roughly chopped
1 zucchini (courgette), thickly sliced
1 small onion, cut into wedges
2 tbs olive oil
140 g (5 oz/²/₃ cup) brown rice (see Note)

185 g (6¹/₂ oz) tin tuna chunks, drained

**orange and basil dressing**
zest of 1 orange
2 tbs orange juice
2 tbs olive oil
3 tbs torn basil leaves

Preheat the oven to 200°C (400°F/Gas 6). Put the capsicum, zucchini and onion in a baking dish. Pour over the oil, season with salt and black pepper, then toss to coat the vegetables with oil. Bake for 20 minutes or until lightly golden and soft, stirring once or twice during cooking.

Meanwhile, cook the rice according to the packet instructions. Drain well, then rinse under cold water and drain again. Leave to cool in a sieve over a saucepan, fluffing up the grains with a fork occasionally.

While the rice is cooling, put all the orange and basil dressing ingredients in a small bowl and whisk well. Season with salt and black pepper.

Put the cooled rice in a bowl, then stir in the tuna and all the roasted vegetables. Pour over the dressing, gently toss together, and divide the salad between two lunchboxes.

Note: You could also use leftover rice for this recipe. You will need about 280 g (10 oz/1$^1$/$_2$ cups) of cold cooked brown rice.

Makes 2 lunchbox salads

brown rice, tuna and roasted vegetable salad

## spicy tempeh salad

125 g (4¹/₂ oz) spicy tempeh,
    cut into fine strips
2 tsp sesame oil
¹/₂ carrot
¹/₂ large red capsicum (pepper)
8 snowpeas (mangetout), tailed
3–4 spring onions (scallions)
75 g (2¹/₂ oz/1 cup) shredded
    red cabbage

1 tbs toasted sesame seeds
60 g (2 oz) crispy fried Chinese
    noodles

### lime and chilli dressing

1 garlic clove, crushed
2 tsp sweet chilli sauce
1 tbs lime juice
1¹/₂ tbs vegetable oil

Preheat the oven to 200°C (400°F/Gas 6). Put the tempeh on a non-stick baking tray, brush lightly with the oil and bake for 20 minutes.

Cut the carrot, capsicum, snowpeas and spring onions into julienne strips and toss in a bowl with the tempeh, cabbage and sesame seeds. Whisk the dressing ingredients together in a small bowl, then drizzle over the salad. Toss to combine, then divide between two lunchboxes. Pack the noodles separately and mix through the salad just before eating.

Makes 2 lunchbox salads

## salami pasta salad

1 baby fennel bulb, trimmed
1/2 small red capsicum (pepper),
   thinly sliced
1/2 green capsicum (pepper),
   thinly sliced
1 celery stalk, sliced
1/2 small red onion, thinly sliced
50 g (1 3/4 oz) thickly sliced
   pepper-coated salami
1 tbs chopped flat-leaf
   (Italian) parsley

100 g (3 1/2 oz) mixed coloured
   fettucine, broken into
   short pieces

dressing
1 1/2 tbs olive oil
3 tsp lemon juice
2 tsp Dijon mustard
1/4 tsp sugar
1 small garlic clove, crushed

Cut the fennel bulb in half, then slice thinly. Toss in a bowl with the capsicum, celery and onion. Cut the salami into strips and add to the salad along with the parsley.

Cook the pasta in a large pot of rapidly boiling salted water until al dente. Drain, rinse under cold water, then drain again. Add to the salad and gently toss everything together. Whisk the dressing ingredients in a small bowl and season with salt and plenty of cracked pepper. Pour over the salad, toss well to coat, then divide between two lunchboxes.

Makes 2 lunchbox salads

A handful of nuts, some gourmet mushrooms and fresh, fiery ginger turn plain noodles into a sumptuous lunchtime surprise.

## buckwheat noodle salad with shiitake and snowpeas

125 g (4$^1$/$_2$ oz) buckwheat noodles
2 tbs walnut pieces
1 tbs vegetable or olive oil
60 g (2$^1$/$_4$ oz) fresh shiitake mushrooms, stalks discarded, caps thinly sliced
50 g (1$^3$/$_4$ oz/$^1$/$_2$ cup) snowpeas, tailed and finely sliced
3 spring onions (scallions), finely sliced

### sesame ginger dressing
1 tbs white wine vinegar
$^1$/$_2$ tsp sesame oil
2 tbs vegetable oil
2 cm ($^3$/$_4$ inch) piece of ginger, peeled and finely grated
1 small red chilli, seeded and finely chopped

Cook the noodles according to the packet instructions. Drain well, then rinse under cold running water, rubbing the noodles together gently to remove some of the starch. Drain well, then place in a bowl.

Meanwhile, put a frying pan over high heat. Add the walnuts and dry-fry for 2–3 minutes, shaking the pan now and then so the nuts colour evenly. Remove, leave to cool and roughly chop.

Heat the oil in the same pan, add the mushrooms and sauté for about 2–3 minutes, or until tender. Add them to the noodles with the snowpeas, spring onion and chopped walnuts and gently mix together.

To make the sesame ginger dressing, put the vinegar, sesame oil and vegetable oil in a small bowl and whisk until well combined. Stir in the ginger and chilli, then drizzle over the noodles. Toss to combine, then divide the noodles between two lunchboxes. Eat at room temperature.

Makes 2 lunchbox salads

buckwheat noodle salad with shiitake and snowpeas

## tuna, capsicum and pasta salad

165 g (5³/4 oz) conchiglie or
   other pasta shells
65 g (2¹/4 oz) green beans,
   trimmed and chopped
1 small red capsicum (pepper),
   thinly sliced
1 spring onion (scallion), sliced
1 large cucumber, thinly sliced
6 hard-boiled eggs, peeled
   and quartered
4 tomatoes, cut into eighths

185 g (6¹/2 oz) tin tuna chunks,
   drained
80 g (2³/4 oz/¹/2 cup) black olives
2 tbs chopped basil

dressing
1 tbs olive oil
3 tbs white wine vinegar
1 tbs lemon juice
1 garlic clove, crushed
1 tsp sugar

Cook the pasta in a large pot of rapidly boiling salted water until al dente, adding the beans for the final minute of cooking. Drain, rinse under cold water and drain again. Place in a large bowl with the capsicum and spring onion and mix well. Add the cucumber, egg, tomato and tuna.

Combine all the dressing ingredients in a small screw-top jar and shake well. Drizzle half the dressing over the salad, then scatter the olives and basil over the top. Divide the salad between two lunchboxes and drizzle with the remaining dressing.

Makes 2 lunchbox salads

## pastrami, mushroom and cucumber salad

100 g (3¹/2 oz) lasagnette
   (mini lasagne sheets),
   broken into quarters
125 g (4¹/2 oz) sliced pastrami,
   cut into strips
¹/2 celery stalk, sliced
1 tomato, cut into wedges
¹/2 Lebanese (short) cucumber,
   thinly sliced
40 g (1¹/2 oz) button
   mushrooms, thinly sliced

¹/2 tablespoon finely chopped
   coriander (cilantro)

dressing
1¹/2 tbs olive oil
1 tablespoon red wine vinegar
¹/2 tsp Dijon mustard
1 garlic clove, crushed
a few drops of chilli oil

Cook the pasta in a large pot of rapidly boiling salted water until al dente. Drain, rinse under cold water and drain again. Allow to cool, then place in a large bowl with the pastrami, celery, tomato, cucumber and mushrooms.

Combine all the dressing ingredients in a small screw-top jar and shake well. Toss the dressing through the salad, then cover and refrigerate for several hours to allow all the flavours to mingle. Adjust the seasoning, then divide between two lunchboxes and sprinkle with the coriander.

Makes 2 lunchbox salads

For hungry days this hearty salad is substantial but not too heavy, enlivened with green beans, fresh tomatoes and olives.

## mediterranean potato salad

2 eggs
125 g (4$^1$/$_2$ oz) green beans, trimmed and cut into 3 cm (1$^1$/$_4$ inch) lengths
300 g (10$^1$/$_2$ oz) waxy potatoes
100 g (3$^1$/$_2$ oz) penne, fusilli or other pasta (see Note)
2 firm, ripe tomatoes, seeded and diced

40 g (1$^1$/$_2$ oz/$^1$/$_4$ cup) Kalamata olives

### anchovy dressing
3 tbs olive oil
1 tbs white wine vinegar
1 garlic clove, crushed
2 anchovy fillets, finely chopped

Bring a small saucepan of water to the boil. Add the eggs and cook for 7 minutes. Add the green beans and cook for a further 2 minutes. Drain the eggs and beans and rinse under cold water. Leave to cool completely.

Meanwhile, put the potatoes in a pot of salted water and bring to the boil. Cook for about 12 minutes, or until the potatoes are tender when

pierced with the tip of a sharp knife. Leave to cool slightly, then cut the potatoes into chunks and place in a large bowl.

Bring a separate pot of salted water to the boil and cook the pasta until al dente. Drain well, then add to the potatoes.

To make the anchovy dressing, whisk the oil and vinegar in a small bowl until well combined. Stir in the garlic and season with a little black pepper. Mash the anchovy into the dressing, mixing well. Pour the dressing over the potatoes and pasta while they are still warm and toss gently.

Peel the eggs and chop them into quarters. Add to the pasta with the beans, tomato and olives. Mix gently and leave to cool completely, then divide the salad between two lunchboxes.

Note: You could use 220 g (8 oz/1 1/4 cups) of leftover cooked pasta instead.

Makes 2 lunchbox salads

mediterranean potato salad

## lemon and vegetable pasta salad

100 g (3¹/₂ oz) farfalle or
    other bow-shaped pasta
1 tbs olive oil
125 g (4¹/₂ oz) broccoli, cut
    into small florets
60 g (2¹/₄ oz) snowpeas
    (mangetout), tailed
75 g (2¹/₂ oz) small yellow
    button squash, quartered

¹/₂ celery stalk, finely sliced
2 tsp chopped chervil
8 chervil sprigs

dressing
1 tbs sour cream
2 tsp lemon juice
1 tbs olive oil
1 tsp finely grated lemon zest

300

Cook the pasta in a large pot of rapidly boiling salted water until al dente. Drain well, toss with 1 tablespoon of the oil and set aside to cool.

Put the broccoli, snowpeas and squash in a large bowl, cover with boiling water and leave for 2 minutes. Drain, plunge into iced water, then drain again. Pat dry with paper towels and gently toss in a large bowl with the pasta and celery. Sprinkle the chopped chervil over the top.

Put all the dressing ingredients in a screw-top jar and shake well. Season to taste, then drizzle over the pasta and toss well. Divide between two lunchboxes and scatter with chervil. Eat at room temperature.

Makes 2 lunchbox salads

# chef's salad

20 g (3/4 oz) Swiss cheese,
  cut into thin strips
2 thin slices of leg ham
75 g (2 1/2 oz) cooked chopped
  chicken or turkey
1 Roma (plum) tomato,
  quartered

1 tbs chopped pimiento
  (see Note)
1 hard-boiled egg, peeled
  and quartered
2 well-shaped lettuce leaves
3 tbs ready-made French
  dressing

Put the cheese, ham, chicken, tomato, pimiento and egg in a bowl and gently toss to combine.

Wash and dry the lettuce leaves thoroughly. Arrange the salad inside the lettuce leaves and carefully place in two lunchboxes. Pack the dressing separately and drizzle over the salad just before eating.

Note: Pimiento is a type of sweet red capsicum (pepper). It is often sold in small jars in delicatessens, speciality shops and some large greengrocers.

Makes 2 lunchbox salads

Zinging with lime, fresh herbs and chilli, this wonderful salad is a true pick-me-up after a dull morning.

## chicken noodle salad

100 g (3¹/₂ oz) bean vermicelli noodles
1 tbs vegetable oil
1 garlic clove, crushed
3 cm (1¹/₄ inch) piece of fresh ginger, peeled and finely grated
1 green chilli, seeded and finely chopped
250 g (9 oz) minced (ground) chicken thighs
2 tbs lemon juice
2 makrut (kaffir lime) leaves, shredded
1 tbs fish sauce
1 tbs chilli sauce
2 tbs chopped coriander (cilantro) leaves

Put the noodles in a large heatproof bowl, cover with boiling water and soak for 5 minutes, or until softened. Alternatively, cook the noodles according to the packet instructions. Drain the noodles well, then rinse under cold water and drain again.

Heat the oil in a wok or frying pan over medium heat. Add the garlic, ginger and chilli and stir-fry for about 1 minute, being careful not to burn the garlic. Add the chicken and stir-fry for another 2–3 minutes. Stir in the lemon juice, lime leaves, fish sauce and chilli sauce and stir-fry for a further minute. Remove from the heat and transfer to a large bowl.

Cut the noodles into shorter lengths with scissors. Add to the chicken mixture along with the coriander and mix well. Leave to cool completely, then divide between two lunchboxes.

Makes 2 lunchbox salads

chicken noodle salad

# caesar salad

dressing
1 egg
1 garlic clove, crushed
1 anchovy fillet
1/4 tsp Worcestershire sauce
3 tsp lime juice
1/2 tsp Dijon mustard
185 ml (6 fl oz/3/4 cup) olive oil

10 g (1/4 oz) butter
2 tsp olive oil
1 slice thick white bread, crust
   removed, cut into cubes
1 rasher of back bacon or
   rindless middle bacon
2 baby cos (romaine) lettuces,
   leaves washed and torn
35 g (11/4 oz/1/3 cup) shaved
   Parmesan cheese

To make the dressing, blend the egg, garlic, anchovy, Worcestershire sauce, lime juice and mustard in a food processor until smooth. With the motor running, add the oil in a thin, steady stream until creamy. Season well.

Heat the butter and oil in a frying pan. Fry the bread over medium heat until crisp, about 5–8 minutes, then remove. Cook the bacon in the same pan for 3 minutes or until crispy, then break into bite-sized pieces.

Divide the lettuce between two lunchboxes and scatter with the Parmesan. Pack the dressing in a separate container, and the bacon and croutons in another container. Add them to the salad just before eating.

Makes 2 lunchbox salads

# chicken, pear and pasta salad

125 g (4¹/2 oz) gemelli, fusilli
    or other spiral pasta
100 g (3¹/2 oz) chicken breast
    fillet
1 pear, cored and thinly sliced
2 spring onions (scallions), finely
    sliced, plus extra, to serve

1 tbs toasted slivered almonds
50 g (1³/4 oz) creamy blue
    cheese
1¹/2 tbs sour cream

Cook the pasta in a large pot of rapidly boiling salted water until al dente. Drain, rinse under cold water and drain again. Allow to cool.

Put the chicken in a frying pan, cover with cold water and simmer gently for 8 minutes, or until tender, turning occasionally. Remove from the pan, allow to cool, then slice finely and place in a bowl with the cooled pasta. Add the pear, spring onion and almonds.

Put the blue cheese and sour cream in a food processor with a large pinch each of salt and pepper and 1¹/2 tablespoons of ice-cold water. Blend until smooth. Pour the mixture over the salad and gently toss to coat. Divide between two lunchboxes and scatter with a few slivers of spring onion.

Makes 2 lunchbox salads

Caramelized leek and lightly melted crumbs of creamy blue cheese lend a savoury sophistication to this simple pasta dish.

## pasta salad with caramelized vegetables

2 tbs olive oil
2 celery stalks, sliced
1 small onion, halved and
thinly sliced
1 garlic clove, crushed
pinch of sugar
2 leeks, white part only, sliced
175 g (6 oz) pasta shells or
bows (see Note)
2 tbs toasted pine nuts

70 g (2¹/₂ oz) soft blue cheese,
such as gorgonzola, crumbled

dressing
1 tbs olive oil
1 tbs chopped flat-leaf (Italian)
parsley
1 tbs lemon juice

Heat the oil in a frying pan. Add the celery and onion, then cover and cook over medium heat for 5 minutes, stirring occasionally. Stir in the garlic, sugar and leek. Reduce the heat, cover the pan and gently cook, stirring occasionally, for a further 10 minutes, or until the vegetables are golden brown and soft. Remove the lid, increase the heat and cook the vegetables for another 2–3 minutes or until light golden, being careful not to burn them. Season with salt and black pepper, then set aside.

Meanwhile, cook the pasta in a large pot of rapidly boiling salted water until al dente. Drain well, then while the pasta is still warm, add the caramelized vegetables and set aside.

Put the dressing ingredients in a small bowl, season with salt and black pepper and mix well. Pour over the pasta, stir in the pine nuts and cheese and toss gently. Leave to cool, then divide between two lunchboxes. This salad is delicious cold, or equally delicious warmed up in a microwave.

Note: To save time, you could use 385 g (13$^1$/$_2$ oz/about 2$^1$/$_4$ cups) of cooked left-over pasta instead.

Makes 2 lunchbox salads

pasta salad with caramelized vegetables

## asparagus and orange salad

175 g (6 oz/1 bunch) thin
   asparagus spears
30 g (1 oz/1 cup) picked
   watercress leaves
1/4 small red onion, very
   thinly sliced
1 small orange, peeled and
   cut into 12 segments
50 g (1 3/4 oz) soft goat's cheese

**orange poppy seed dressing**
1/2 tbs orange juice
1/2 tsp finely grated orange zest
1/2 tsp sugar
1/2 tbs red wine vinegar
1 tsp poppy seeds
1 tbs olive oil

Bring a pot of lightly salted water to the boil, add the asparagus and blanch for 1–2 minutes or until bright green and just tender. Drain and refresh under cold water, then drain again.

Gently toss the asparagus in a bowl with the watercress, onion and orange segments. Divide the salad between two lunchboxes and crumble the goat's cheese over the top. Season to taste with salt and pepper.

To make the orange poppy seed dressing, mix together the orange juice, orange zest, sugar, vinegar and poppy seeds, then whisk in the oil. Pack the dressing separately and drizzle over the salad just before eating.

Makes 2 lunchbox salads

## cucumber, feta, mint and dill salad

2 Lebanese (short) cucumbers
100 g (3$^1$/$_2$ oz) feta cheese, cubed
$^1$/$_2$ small red onion, thinly sliced
3 tsp finely chopped dill
$^1$/$_2$ tbs dried mint
1$^1$/$_2$ tbs olive oil
3 tsp lemon juice

Peel the cucumbers, scoop out the seeds, then cut the flesh into 1 cm ($^1$/$_2$ inch) cubes. Gently toss in a bowl with the feta, onion and dill.

Grind the mint to a powder in a mortar and pestle, or force it through a sieve. Place in a small bowl with the oil and lemon juice, then season with salt and black pepper and mix well. Drizzle the dressing over the salad, toss well, then divide between two lunchboxes.

Makes 2 lunchbox salads

This inventive way with chicken, corn and rice shows you need never compromise on quality if you're in a hurry.

## rice salad with chicken

150 g (5½ oz/¾ cup) jasmine rice (see Note)
100 g (3½ oz) roast or barbecued chicken
½ Lebanese (short) cucumber, seeded and diced
250 g (9 oz/1 punnet) grape tomatoes, halved
4 spring onions (scallions), sliced
310 g (11 oz) tin corn kernels, drained

### dressing
3 tbs olive oil
1 tbs lemon juice
1 tbs runny honey
1 tsp Dijon mustard
1 small red chilli, seeded and sliced

Cook the rice in a large pot of boiling water until just tender. Drain well, briefly rinse under cold water, then drain again. Leave in a sieve over a saucepan, fluffing up the grains occasionally with a fork. While the rice is still warm, place it in a bowl while you make the dressing.

Whisk all the dressing ingredients together thoroughly in a small bowl, season with salt and black pepper and pour over the warm rice. Mix well, then cover and refrigerate until cooled completely.

Shred the chicken into bite-sized pieces and mix through the rice with the cucumber, tomato, spring onion and corn kernels. Check the seasoning, then divide between two lunchboxes.

Note: You could use 440 g (1 lb/2$^1$/$_4$ cups) of cold cooked rice instead.

Makes 2 lunchbox salads

rice salad with chicken

**warm winter**  Long cold evenings and chilly weekends stoke up the appetite for good square meals that will warm you up without weighing you down. So when the mercury starts dropping, fire up your enthusiasm and head straight for the kitchen. Whip on your apron, crank up your creativity, rustle up a wonderful warm salad and before long you'll feel a glow of contentment from top to toe.

The concept of cold and raw may be refreshing and appealing when the temperature is soaring and eating can seem a chore. But as the nights draw in ever earlier and you find yourself ferreting for last year's jumpers and thick woolly socks it takes a little something extra to make a satisfying meal. Roasts, stews and bakes naturally have their place in any winter repertoire, but satisfying doesn't have to mean stodgy. Weekend lunches, dinner for one and late-night meals after a long day at work are the prime times when many of us sneak off to the nearest takeaway shop or settle for the short-lived comfort of baked beans on toast in front of the television. But when preparing a full-blown meal seems off-putting and it's tempting to take to the couch and reach for the phone to order a lard-laden home delivery, don't despair: this is when the warm salad comes into its own. Healthy rather than worthy, the best warm salads take the finest produce of the season and turn winter's harvest into delectable, satisfying meals that nourish the soul as well as the body. Comfort food comes in all shapes and sizes and warm salads deserve to figure highly on the list. This is seriously good food that needn't involve an assembly line of ingredients and cooks. Warm, salty prosciutto, oozy melted cheese and fresh, delicate greens are all the more enticing when quickly cooked. Roasting root vegetables, onions and garlic brings a mellow warmth and caramelized sweetness that is infinitely soothing on a cold, dark evening — and as an added bonus, the hot oven turns a cold house into a cosy cocoon filled with heartening aromas. So it's time to welcome in food that is deeply invigorating — a celebration of winter and the opportunity for reflection and quiet contemplation that it brings.

## scallop salad with saffron dressing

**saffron dressing**
pinch of saffron threads
60 g (2¼ oz/¼ cup)
   ready-made mayonnaise
1½ tbs cream
1 tsp lemon juice

20 scallops, with roe
25 g (1 oz) butter
1 tbs olive oil
100 g (3½ oz) mixed salad
   leaves
1 small handful chervil leaves

To make the saffron dressing, put the saffron in a bowl and soak in 2 teaspoons of hot water for 10 minutes. Add the mayonnaise, mixing well, until the mixture becomes rich yellow in colour. Stir in the cream, then the lemon juice. Refrigerate until needed.

Slice or pull off any vein, membrane or hard white muscle from the scallops, leaving the roe attached. Rinse the scallops and pat them dry with paper towels. Heat the butter and oil in a large frying pan over high heat and sear the scallops in small batches for 1 minute on each side.

Divide the salad leaves and chervil between four serving plates, then top each with five scallops. Drizzle the dressing over the top and serve.

Serves 4

## scallop and potato with preserved lemon dressing

preserved lemon dressing
1/2 preserved lemon
3 tbs olive oil
2 tbs lemon juice
1 tbs sweet chilli sauce
2 tbs white wine vinegar
2 tbs chopped coriander
    (cilantro)

oil, for pan-frying
500 g (1 lb 2 oz) potatoes,
    peeled and sliced paper thin
750 g (1 lb 10 oz) scallops,
    without roe
75 g (2 1/2 oz) baby English
    spinach leaves

First, make the dressing. Scoop out and discard the pulp from the preserved lemon, wash the rind well and thinly slice it. Place in a bowl with the remaining dressing ingredients and whisk together well.

Heat 2 cm (3/4 inch) of oil in a deep heavy-based frying pan and cook the potato in batches over medium heat for 1–2 minutes, or until crisp and golden. Drain on crumpled paper towels.

Rinse the scallops and pat them dry. Heat some oil in a frying pan and cook the scallops in batches over high heat for 1 minute on each side, until golden. Serve on a bed of spinach and potato, drizzled with the dressing.

Serves 4

Tender quarters of artichoke heart enveloped in crispy, golden breadcrumbs make this dish an adorable winter treat.

## prosciutto and rocket with parmesan-crusted artichoke

4 globe artichokes
1 lemon, halved
2 eggs, lightly beaten
20 g (3/4 oz/1/4 cup) fresh
   breadcrumbs
25 g (1 oz/1/4 cup) grated
   Parmesan cheese
oil, for pan-frying

1 tbs olive oil
8 slices of prosciutto
3 tsp white wine vinegar
1 garlic clove, crushed
150 g (51/2 oz/1 bunch) rocket
   (arugula), trimmed
shaved Parmesan cheese,
   to serve

Remove the tough outer leaves from the artichokes, down to the pale leaves. Slice off the tops, halfway down the tough leaves. Trim the stems to 4 cm (11/2 inches) long, then peel lightly. Halve each artichoke lengthways and remove the hairy choke with a teaspoon. Rub the artichokes with the lemon while you work and place in a bowl of cold water mixed with lemon juice to stop them turning brown. Cut them into quarters, place in a large pot of boiling water and cook for 2 minutes, then drain.

Whisk the eggs in a bowl, and combine the seasoned breadcrumbs and grated Parmesan in another bowl. Dip each artichoke quarter into the egg, then roll in the breadcrumb mixture to coat.

Heat 2 cm (3/4 inch) of oil in a deep heavy-based frying pan. Add the artichokes in batches and fry over medium heat for 2–3 minutes, or until golden. Remove and drain on crumpled paper towels.

Heat the olive oil in a non-stick frying pan. Cook the prosciutto in two batches over medium heat for 2 minutes, or until crisp. Remove the prosciutto with tongs, leaving the oil in the pan. Mix the vinegar and garlic into the pan oil with a little salt and pepper to use as a dressing.

Put the rocket in a bowl, add half the dressing and toss well. Divide the rocket, artichokes and prosciutto between four plates and drizzle with the remaining dressing. Scatter with Parmesan, sprinkle with sea salt and serve.

Serves 4

scallop salad with saffron dressing

## scallop salad with lime and ginger

dressing
3 tbs peanut oil
1 tbs lime juice
1 tbs grated fresh ginger
1/2 tsp honey
1 tbs chopped coriander
   (cilantro)

3 zucchini (courgettes), julienned
2 carrots, julienned
2 spring onions (scallions),
   sliced on the diagonal
400 g (14 oz) scallops,
   without roe
1 tbs peanut oil

Put all the dressing ingredients in a small screw-top jar and shake well. Arrange the zucchini, carrot and spring onion on four serving plates.

Slice or pull off any vein, membrane or hard white muscle from the scallops. Rinse the scallops and pat them dry with paper towels.

Heat the oil in a heavy-based pan. Add the scallops and cook in small batches over high heat for 1 minute on each side, or until golden. Remove from the pan and keep warm while cooking the remaining batches.

Pile the scallops over the vegetables, drizzle with the dressing and serve.

Serves 4

## thai-style chicken salad

4 chicken breast fillets, cut
    into 1 cm (1/2 inch) strips
1 tsp grated fresh ginger
1 garlic clove, crushed
2 tbs soy sauce
1 tbs peanut oil
3 spring onions (scallions),
    sliced diagonally

2 carrots, julienned
35 g (1 1/4 oz) snowpea
    (mangetout) sprouts

### dressing
2 tbs sweet chilli sauce
1 tbs rice vinegar
2 tbs peanut oil

Put the chicken in a non-metallic dish. Mix together the ginger, garlic and soy sauce and smother the mixture all over the chicken. Cover and refrigerate for at least 2 hours — preferably overnight — turning occasionally.

Nearer to serving time, put all the dressing ingredients in a small screw-top jar and shake well.

Heat the oil in a heavy-based pan. Add the chicken and cook in batches over medium heat for 3–4 minutes, or until cooked and nicely browned. Drain on crumpled paper towels and set aside to cool, then place in a serving bowl with the spring onion, carrot and snowpea sprouts. Pour the dressing over the top and toss lightly to combine. Serve immediately.

Serves 4

Soft and gooey, warm and salty, pan-fried haloumi is heavenly piled high on crusty, buttery garlic bread.

## haloumi salad and warm garlic bread

4 firm ripe tomatoes
1 Lebanese (short) cucumber
150 g (5½ oz/1 bunch) rocket
   (arugula), trimmed
95 g (3 oz/½ cup) Kalamata
   olives
1 whole loaf crusty white bread
2 tbs olive oil
1 large garlic clove, cut in half

400 g (14 oz) haloumi cheese,
   cut into 8 slices

dressing
1 tbs lemon juice
1 tbs chopped fresh oregano
3 tbs olive oil

Cut the tomatoes and cucumber into bite-sized chunks and toss in a serving dish with the rocket and olives. Mix well.

Whisk together the dressing ingredients in a small bowl, season to taste with salt and freshly cracked pepper and set aside.

Slice the bread into eight 1.5 cm ($^5$/$_8$ inch) slices. Drizzle the bread with 1$^1$/$_2$ tablespoons of the oil and season with salt and pepper. Cook under a hot griller (broiler) for about 1–2 minutes on each side, or until lightly golden, then thoroughly rub each slice with a cut side of the garlic. Wrap the bread loosely in foil and keep in a warm oven.

Heat the remaining oil in a frying pan and fry the haloumi over medium heat for 1–2 minutes on each side, or until golden brown.

Pour half the dressing over the salad and toss well. Arrange the haloumi on top and drizzle with the rest of the dressing. Serve immediately with the warm garlic bread.

Serves 4

thai-style chicken salad

## roasted mushroom and goat's cheese salad

6 large-cap mushrooms,
   stems removed
3 tsp chopped thyme
3 garlic cloves, finely chopped
1¹/2 tbs olive oil
50 g (1³/4 oz) baby rocket
   (arugula) leaves
100 g (3¹/2 oz) goat's cheese

1¹/2 tbs chopped flat-leaf
   (Italian) parsley

**lemon dressing**
1¹/2 tbs lemon juice
2 tbs olive oil
¹/2 tsp grated lemon zest

Preheat the oven to 200°C (400°F/Gas 6). Put the mushrooms on a large baking tray, sprinkle with the thyme and garlic, then drizzle with the oil. Cover with foil and roast for 20 minutes. Take the mushrooms out of the oven, give them a good toss to mix the flavours through, then put the foil back on and roast for a further 10 minutes, or until cooked.

Meanwhile, put the dressing ingredients in a small bowl and whisk well.

Spread the rocket on a serving platter. Cut the mushrooms in half and arrange them over the rocket. Crumble the goat's cheese over the top, give the dressing another quick whisk and drizzle it over the salad. Sprinkle with parsley and serve while warm.

Serves 4

## goat's cheese toasts with rocket salad

12 slices white bread
4 rounds of goat's cheese
60 g (2¼ oz) mixed salad leaves
60 g (2¼ oz/½ small bunch)
    rocket (arugula), trimmed
250 g (9 oz/1 punnet) cherry
    tomatoes, halved
1 tbs snipped chives

dressing
1 tbs white wine vinegar
3 tbs olive oil
½ tsp wholegrain mustard

Preheat the oven to 180°C (350°F/Gas 4). Use a biscuit cutter the same size as the goat's cheese to cut a round out of each slice of bread. (The bread needs to be the same diameter as the cheese so the edges won't burn.) Put the bread on a baking tray and bake for 10 minutes.

Slice each piece of goat's cheese into three rounds, then place a slice on each piece of toasted bread. Cook under a hot grill (broiler) for 5 minutes, or until the cheese turns golden and bubbles.

Arrange the salad greens and cherry tomatoes on four small serving plates. Whisk the dressing ingredients in a small jug and drizzle over the salad. Arrange three cheese rounds on each plate, scatter with chives and serve.

Serves 4

Toasted hazelnut and sweet, juicy orange make this simple salad an appetizing base for meltingly warm goat's cheese.

## warm goat's cheese salad with orange and hazelnut

hazelnut dressing
20 g (3/4 oz) hazelnuts
1 tbs orange juice
1 tbs lemon juice
125 ml (4 fl oz/1/2 cup)
    olive oil

2 oranges
250 g (9 oz/1/2 bunch)
    watercress, picked
50 g (13/4 oz) baby English
    spinach leaves
olive oil, for brushing
300 g (101/2 oz) goat's cheese,
    sliced into 4 portions

Preheat the oven to 180°C (350°F/Gas 4). To make the dressing, put the hazelnuts on a baking tray and roast for 5–6 minutes, or until the skins turn dark brown. Wrap the hazelnuts in a clean tea towel and rub them together to remove the skins, then put them in a food processor with the orange juice, lemon juice and a pinch of salt. With the motor running, gradually add the oil a few drops at a time. When about half the oil has been incorporated, add the remainder in a steady stream.

Peel the rind and bitter white pith from the oranges. Cut the flesh into segments between the membrane, removing the seeds. Put the segments in a large bowl with the watercress, spinach and 2 tablespoons of the dressing. Toss well and season to taste with pepper.

Heat a small, non-stick frying pan and brush lightly with olive oil. Carefully press each slice of goat's cheese firmly into the pan and cook over medium heat for 1–2 minutes, or until a crust forms underneath.

Arrange half the salad over four serving plates and put the goat's cheese slices on top, crust-side-up. Scatter with the remaining salad, drizzle with the remaining dressing and serve at once.

Serves 4

warm goat's cheese salad with orange and hazelnut

## spinach salad with bacon and quail eggs

12 quail eggs

2 1/2 tbs oil

4 rashers of back bacon or
   middle rashers, cut into
   thin strips

2 tbs apple cider vinegar

2 garlic cloves, crushed

1 tsp Dijon mustard

1 tsp maple syrup

1/2 tsp Worcestershire sauce

250 g (9 oz) baby English
   spinach leaves

200 g (7 oz) cherry tomatoes,
   halved

50 g (1 3/4 oz/1/3 cup) toasted
   pine nuts

Bring a small saucepan of water to the boil. Carefully add the quail eggs and simmer for 1 1/2 minutes. Drain, then refresh under cold running water until cool. Carefully peel the eggs and cut them in half.

Heat a little of the oil in a non-stick frying pan. Add the bacon and gently cook for 5 minutes, or until crisp. Remove with tongs, leaving the oil behind, and drain on crumpled paper towels. Add the vinegar, garlic, mustard, maple syrup and Worcestershire sauce to the pan and gently swirl for 2 minutes, or until bubbling. Add the remaining oil and heat for 1 minute.

Layer the spinach, bacon, tomatoes and pine nuts in a salad bowl. Add the quail eggs, pour the warm dressing over, season to taste and serve.

Serves 4

## ricotta toasts with pear and walnut salad

1 small baguette, cut into
   16 thin slices
oil, for brushing
1 garlic clove, cut in half
100 g (3<sup>1</sup>/2 oz/1 cup) walnuts
2 pears, cored and diced
2 tbs lime juice

400 g (14 oz) mixed salad leaves
200 g (7 oz) ricotta cheese

**lime vinaigrette**
3 tbs lime juice
3 tbs oil
2 tbs raspberry vinegar

Preheat the oven to 180°C (350°F/Gas 4). Brush the bread with a little oil, rub with the cut sides of the garlic, spread on a baking tray and bake for 10 minutes, or until golden. Bake the walnuts for 5 minutes, or until lightly browned, turning to ensure even colouring. Cool for 5 minutes.

Whisk the lime vinaigrette ingredients in a small bowl with 1 teaspoon salt and <sup>1</sup>/2 teaspoon freshly ground black pepper. Put the pear cubes in a bowl, add the lime juice and mix well. Add the vinaigrette, salad leaves and walnuts, toss well, then divide between four serving bowls.

Spread the bread toasts with ricotta and cook under a hot griller (broiler) for 2–3 minutes, or until hot. Arrange four slices on each plate and serve.

Serves 4

These tantalizingly tender slices of perfectly pink, peppery lamb
are almost worth sacrificing summer for.

### greek peppered lamb salad

1 1/2 tbs black pepper
300 g (10 1/2 oz) lamb backstraps
    or loin fillets
1 tbs olive oil
3 vine-ripened tomatoes,
    each cut into 8 wedges
2 Lebanese (short) cucumbers,
    sliced
150 g (5 1/2 oz) marinated
    Kalamata olives, drained
    (reserve 1 1/2 tbs of the oil
    for the dressing)

100 g (3 1/2 oz) feta cheese,
    cut into cubes
1/2 tsp dried oregano

dressing
1/4 tsp dried oregano
1 tbs lemon juice
1 tbs extra virgin olive oil

Scatter the pepper in a small shallow dish large enough to hold the lamb.
Roll the lamb around in the pepper, pressing the pepper on with your
fingers. Cover and refrigerate for 15 minutes.

Heat the oil in a frying pan or chargrill pan (griddle). Cook the lamb over high heat for 2–3 minutes on each side, or until cooked to your liking. Remove from the heat, cover with foil and keep in a warm place.

Gently toss the tomato, cucumber, olives, feta and oregano together in a bowl. Put the dressing ingredients in a small bowl, add the reserved oil from the olives and whisk well. Season to taste, then pour half the dressing over the salad. Toss well, then arrange on a serving platter.

Cut the lamb on the diagonal into 1 cm ($^1/_2$ inch) thick slices and arrange on top of the salad. Pour the remaining dressing over the top and serve.

Serves 4

spinach salad with bacon and quail eggs

## broad bean, mint and bacon salad

600 g (1 lb 5 oz) frozen broad
   (fava) beans, defrosted
250 g (9 oz) piece of Kasseler
   or pancetta (see Note)
1 tbs olive oil
1/2 butter lettuce, shredded
2 large handfuls mint, shredded
4 flatbreads

**dressing**
1 1/2 tsp Dijon mustard
1 tsp sugar
2 tbs white wine vinegar
3 tbs extra virgin olive oil

Cook the beans in a pot of lightly salted boiling water for 2–3 minutes, or until tender. Drain, refresh under cold water and remove the skins.

Slice the Kasseler or pancetta into 2 cm (3/4 inch) chunks. Heat the oil in a heavy-based frying pan and fry on all sides for 3–4 minutes, or until golden. Toss in a large bowl with the beans, lettuce and mint.

To make the dressing, combine the mustard, sugar and vinegar in a jug. Whisk in the oil and season to taste. Pile the salad onto fresh or lightly toasted flatbreads, drizzle with dressing and serve.

Note: Kasseler is a German smoked pork loin sold in good delicatessens.

Serves 4

## warm potato salad with green olive dressing

1 kg (2 lb 4 oz) small, waxy
    potatoes (such as nicola),
    scrubbed

### green olive dressing
60 g (2¼ oz/⅓ cup) green
    olives, pitted and finely
    chopped

1 tsp capers, rinsed, drained
    and finely chopped
1 large handful parsley,
    finely chopped
1½ tbs lemon juice
1 tsp finely grated lemon zest
2 garlic cloves, crushed
4 tbs extra virgin olive oil

Put the potatoes in a pot of cold, lightly salted water. Bring to the boil, then reduce the heat and simmer for 12–15 minutes, or until tender when pierced with a sharp knife. Drain and allow to cool slightly.

While the potatoes are cooking, put all the green olive dressing ingredients in a small bowl and whisk together well with a fork.

While the potatoes are still warm, cut them in half, transfer to a large serving bowl and gently toss the dressing through. Season to taste with fresh black pepper, and a little salt if needed.

Serves 4

Don't grumble when the weather hits an all-time low. This homely, humble salad will cheer the very cockles of your soul.

### sausage and egg salad with anchovy dressing

4 eggs
250 g (9 oz) green beans,
    trimmed and halved
2 tbs olive oil
4 good-quality sausages, cut
    into 1 cm (1/2 inch) slices
2 thick slices crusty white
    bread, crusts removed, cut
    into 1 cm (1/2 inch) cubes
200 g (7 oz) mixed salad leaves

150 g (51/2 oz) roasted red
    capsicum (pepper), sliced

anchovy dressing
1 garlic clove, crushed
3 tbs olive oil
2 tbs lemon juice
3 anchovy fillets, finely chopped
2 tbs shredded basil leaves

Bring a small saucepan of water to the boil, add the eggs and cook for 5 minutes. Add the beans and cook for a further 2 minutes. Drain and rinse the eggs and beans under cold water, draining the beans well. Crack the egg shells slightly and leave to cool in cold water.

Meanwhile, heat half the oil in a frying pan. Add the sausage slices and fry over medium heat for about 5 minutes, or until golden and cooked, turning once. Remove from the pan using a slotted spoon and set aside.

Put the frying pan back over medium heat and add the remaining oil. When the oil is hot, add the bread cubes and fry, turning now and then, for about 2 minutes, or until golden on all sides.

Put all the anchovy dressing ingredients in a small bowl. Mash the anchovies well, mix thoroughly, then season with black pepper and set aside.

Once the eggs have cooled, peel them and then cut them into quarters. Put the sausages, beans, salad leaves and capsicum in a serving bowl. Add the dressing and toss gently. Top with the eggs and croutons and serve.

Serves 4

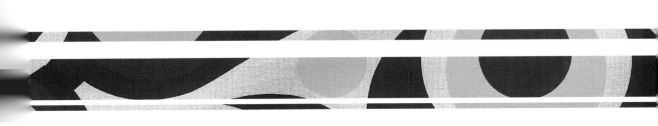

sausage and egg salad with anchovy dressing

## mixed salad with warm brie dressing

½ sourdough baguette
165 ml (5¾ fl oz) olive oil
6 rashers of streaky bacon
2 garlic cloves, peeled
2 baby cos (romaine) lettuces,
    leaves separated
90 g (3¼ oz/2 cups) baby
    English spinach leaves

80 g (2¾ oz/½ cup) toasted
    pine nuts
2 French shallots (eschalots),
    finely chopped
1 tbs Dijon mustard
4 tbs sherry vinegar
300 g (10½ oz) ripe Brie
    cheese, rind removed

Preheat the oven to 180°C (350°F/Gas 4). Thinly slice the baguette and brush each slice all over with some of the oil. Spread on a baking tray and bake for 20 minutes, or until golden. Bake the bacon on a separate tray for 4 minutes, or until crisp, then break into pieces and leave to cool.

Rub the top of each toasted bread slice with one garlic clove, cut in half. Toss in a large bowl with the bacon, lettuce, spinach and pine nuts.

Heat the remaining oil in a frying pan. Add the shallot and gently cook for 1–2 minutes to soften. Crush the remaining garlic clove and add to the pan with the mustard and vinegar. Gently whisk in the Brie until it has melted. Pour the warm dressing over the salad, toss gently and serve.

Serves 4

## roasted tomato, bacon and pasta salad

375 g (13 oz) cherry tomatoes
6 garlic cloves, unpeeled
2 tbs olive oil
400 g (14 oz) pasta
6 rashers (about 125 g/4$\frac{1}{2}$ oz)
  of rindless smoked bacon

150 g (5$\frac{1}{2}$ oz) feta cheese,
  crumbled
80 g (2$\frac{3}{4}$ oz/$\frac{1}{2}$ cup) Kalamata
  olives
1 large handful shredded basil

Preheat the oven to 180°C (350°F/Gas 4). Put the tomatoes and garlic in a roasting dish and drizzle with the oil. Season, toss lightly to coat, then bake for 15–20 minutes (reserve the roasting juices). Meanwhile, cook the pasta in a large pot of rapidly boiling salted water until al dente. Drain well.

Put a non-stick frying pan over high heat. Add the bacon and cook for 4–5 minutes, or until crispy. Remove the bacon with tongs, leaving all the pan juices behind, then chop into strips. Swish some of the pasta around the frying pan to soak up all the pan juices. Season with salt and pepper if needed, then empty into a large serving bowl with the rest of the pasta, the bacon, roasted tomatoes, feta and olives. Toss gently.

Squeeze the garlic cloves from their skins and mix them with the roasted tomato juices. Toss through the pasta, scatter with basil and serve warm.

Serves 4

# beef satay salad

2 tsp tamarind pulp
1/2 tsp sesame oil
2 tbs soy sauce
2 tsp palm sugar or soft
    brown sugar
2 garlic cloves, crushed
1 tbs lime juice
700 g (1 lb 9 oz) rump steak
1 tbs peanut oil
6 large cos (romaine) lettuce
    leaves, shredded
1 red capsicum (pepper),
    julienned
180 g (6 oz/2 cups) bean
    sprouts, tails trimmed
2 tbs crisp fried onion

satay sauce
2 red chillies, chopped
1/2 tsp shrimp paste
1 garlic clove
6 red Asian shallots
2 tsp peanut oil
250 ml (9 fl oz/1 cup) coconut
    milk
1 tbs lime juice
120 g (4 oz/3/4 cup) unsalted
    roasted peanuts, finely
    ground in a food processor
1 tbs kecap manis
1 tbs soft brown sugar
1 tbs fish sauce
2 makrut (kaffir lime) leaves,
    shredded

Mix the tamarind pulp with 3 tablespoons of boiling water, then leave to cool. Mash the pulp with your fingertips to dissolve it, then strain well, reserving the liquid. Discard the pulp.

Put the sesame oil, soy sauce, sugar, garlic, lime juice and 2 tablespoons of the tamarind water in a large non-metallic bowl. Add the beef, turn to coat, then cover with plastic wrap. Chill for 2 hours, turning occasionally.

Meanwhile, make the satay sauce. Put the chillies, shrimp paste, garlic and shallots in a food processor and blend to a paste. Heat the peanut oil in a frying pan and cook the paste over medium heat for 3 minutes. Add the remaining tamarind water and remaining satay sauce ingredients and cook until thickened. Thin with 125 ml (4 fl oz/$^1$/$_2$ cup) water, then return to the boil for 2 minutes. Season to taste.

About 30 minutes before you're ready to eat, remove the beef from the fridge to bring it to room temperature. Heat the peanut oil in a frying pan. Cook the beef over high heat for about 3 minutes on each side, or until medium-rare. Remove from the heat, cover with foil and rest in a warm place for 3 minutes, then thinly slice. Toss in a large bowl with the lettuce, capsicum and bean sprouts. Pile onto serving plates, drizzle with the satay sauce, then sprinkle with fried onion flakes and serve.

Serves 4

roasted tomato, bacon and pasta salad

## spinach and avocado salad with warm mustard

| | |
|---|---|
| 250 g (9 oz/¹/₂ bunch) English spinach | 3 tbs olive oil |
| 1 red or green coral lettuce | 2 tsp sesame seeds |
| 2 small avocados, thinly sliced | 1 tbs lemon juice |
| | 2 tsp wholegrain mustard |

Strip the stalks from the spinach, and discard the outer leaves of the lettuce. Wash and thoroughly dry the spinach and lettuce leaves and tear them into bite-sized pieces. Put them in a large serving bowl and scatter with the avocado slices.

Heat 1 tablespoon of the oil in a small pan. Add the sesame seeds and fry over low heat until they just start to turn golden — this won't take long. Remove from the heat immediately and allow to cool slightly.

Add the remaining oil, lemon juice and mustard to the pan and stir well. Pour the warm dressing over the salad, toss gently to coat the leaves and serve immediately.

Serves 4

# warm butterbean salad

2 tbs olive oil
1 onion, finely chopped
1 garlic clove, crushed
1 small red capsicum (pepper),
 cut into short strips
90 g (3¼ oz) green beans,
 trimmed

8–10 button mushrooms, sliced
1 tbs balsamic vinegar
440 g (14 oz) tin butterbeans
 (lima beans)
chopped parsley, to serve

Heat half the oil in a frying pan. Add the onion and gently stir for about 2 minutes over medium heat. Add the garlic, capsicum, green beans, mushrooms and vinegar, then cook for 5 minutes, stirring occasionally.

Thoroughly rinse and drain the butterbeans. Add them to the pan with the remaining oil and stir until just warmed through. Sprinkle with the chopped parsley and serve.

Serves 4

## prawn and cannellini bean salad

200 g (7 oz/1 cup) dried
    cannellini beans
2 red capsicums (peppers)
300 g (10½ oz) baby green
    beans
½ loaf day-old ciabatta or
    other crusty bread
4 tbs olive oil
1 large garlic clove, finely
    chopped
1 kg (2 lb 4 oz) raw prawns
    (shrimp), peeled and
    deveined, tails intact

1 large handful flat-leaf (Italian)
    parsley, roughly chopped

**lemon and caper dressing**
3 tbs lemon juice
3 tbs olive oil
2 tbs capers, rinsed, drained
    and chopped
1 tsp sugar, optional

Soak the cannellini beans in plenty of cold water for at least 8 hours, or overnight if possible. Drain the beans, rinse them well, then put them in a pot and cover with plenty of fresh, cold water. Bring to the boil, then reduce the heat and simmer for 20–30 minutes, or until tender. Drain, rinse under cold water, then drain again and put in a serving bowl.

Cut the capsicums into large flat pieces and remove the seeds and membranes. Cook, skin-side-up, under a hot grill (broiler) until the skins blacken and blister. Leave to cool in a plastic bag, then peel away the skin and cut the flesh into strips. Add them to the cannellini beans.

Bring a saucepan of lightly salted water to the boil, add the green beans and blanch until bright green and just tender, about 2–3 minutes. Drain and add to the serving bowl.

Put all the lemon and caper dressing ingredients in a screw-top jar and shake well. Season to taste and set aside.

Cut the bread into six slices, then cut each slice into quarters. Heat 3 tablespoons of the oil in a frying pan and fry the bread slices over medium heat for a minute or two on each side until golden. Remove.

Heat the remaining oil in the frying pan, add the garlic and prawns and cook for 2–3 minutes, or until the prawns turn opaque. Toss the prawns through the salad with the dressing, toasted bread and parsley and serve.

Serves 4

prawn and cannellini bean salad

## warm casarecci and sweet potato salad

750 g (1 lb 10 oz) orange
    sweet potato, peeled and
    cut into chunks
2 tbs olive oil
500 g (1 lb 2 oz) casarecci pasta
325 g (11 1/2 oz) jar marinated
    feta cheese, in oil
3 tbs balsamic vinegar

175 g (6 oz/1 bunch) asparagus,
    trimmed and sliced
100 g (3 1/2 oz) baby rocket
    (arugula) or baby English
    spinach leaves
2 ripe tomatoes, chopped
40 g (1 1/2 oz/1/4 cup) toasted
    pine nuts

Preheat the oven to 200°C (400°F/Gas 6). Put the sweet potato in a roasting tin, drizzle with the oil, season liberally and bake for 20 minutes, or until tender. Meanwhile, cook the pasta in a large pot of rapidly boiling salted water until al dente. Drain well and place in a serving bowl.

Drain 3 tablespoons of oil from the feta and whisk it together with the vinegar to make a dressing.

Boil, steam or microwave the asparagus until bright green and just tender. Drain, refresh in cold water and drain again. Add to the pasta with the sweet potato, rocket, feta, tomato and pine nuts. Pour the dressing over and toss gently. Season with black pepper and serve.

Serves 4

## warm artichoke salad

8 young globe artichokes
    (about 200 g/7 oz each)
1 lemon, halved
2¹/₂ handfuls basil leaves,
    shredded
50 g (1³/₄ oz/¹/₂ cup) shaved
    Parmesan cheese

dressing
1 garlic clove, finely chopped
¹/₂ tsp sugar
1 tsp Dijon mustard
2 tsp finely chopped lemon zest
3 tbs lemon juice
4 tbs extra virgin olive oil

Remove the tough outer leaves from the artichokes, down to the pale leaves. Slice off the tops, halfway down the tough leaves. Trim the stems to 4 cm (1¹/₂ inches) long and lightly peel them. Cut the artichokes in half lengthways and remove the hairy choke with a teaspoon. Rub each one with lemon while you work and place in a bowl of cold water mixed with lemon juice to stop them turning brown. Put the artichokes in a large pot of boiling water, top with a plate or heatproof bowl to keep them immersed, then cook for 25 minutes, or until tender. Drain and cut in half.

To make the dressing, mix the garlic, sugar, mustard, lemon zest and lemon juice in a jug. Season with salt and freshly ground black pepper, then whisk in the oil with a fork until combined. Pour over the warm artichoke and scatter with the basil and Parmesan.

Serves 4

The distinctive peppery notes of horseradish, watercress and black pepper strike a sterling chord with subtle, salty salmon.

## pepper-crusted salmon salad

1 tbs coarsely ground black pepper
4 salmon fillets (about 180 g/6 oz each), skin removed
80 g (2³/4 oz/¹/3 cup) ready-made mayonnaise
1¹/2 tbs lemon juice
2 tsp creamed horseradish
1 small garlic clove, crushed
2 tbs chopped parsley
100 g (3¹/2 oz/3 heaped cups) picked watercress
3 tbs olive oil
25 g (1 oz) butter
8 butter lettuce leaves, torn

Mix the pepper in a bowl with ¹/4 teaspoon salt. Use the mixture to coat both sides of each salmon fillet, pressing the pepper down firmly with your fingers. Cover and refrigerate for 30 minutes.

Put the mayonnaise in a food processor with the lemon juice, horseradish, garlic, parsley, half the watercress, 1 tablespoon of the oil and 1 tablespoon of warm water. Blend for 1 minute.

Heat the butter and 1 tablespoon of the oil in a large frying pan until bubbling. Add the salmon fillets and cook over medium heat for about 2–3 minutes on each side for medium-rare, or until cooked to your liking. Remove from the pan and allow to cool slightly.

Arrange the lettuce in the middle of four serving plates and drizzle lightly with the remaining oil. Break each salmon fillet into four pieces and arrange over the lettuce. Scatter the watercress over the top, pour the dressing over and serve at once.

Serves 4

pepper-crusted salmon salad

## eggplant and lentil salad

3 tbs olive oil
1/2 large eggplant (aubergine),
    (about 300 g/10 1/2 oz), cut
    into 5 mm (1/4 inch) cubes
1 small red onion, finely diced
1/4 tsp ground cumin
3 garlic cloves, chopped

200 g (7 oz) Puy or green lentils
375 ml (13 fl oz/1 1/2 cups)
    vegetable stock
2 tbs chopped parsley
1 tbs red wine vinegar
1 tbs extra virgin olive oil

Heat 2 tablespoons of the olive oil in a large frying pan. Add the eggplant and cook over medium heat, stirring constantly, for 5 minutes or until soft. Add the onion and cumin and sauté for 2–3 minutes, or until the onion has softened. Transfer to a serving bowl and season well.

Heat the remaining olive oil in the frying pan. Add the garlic and cook over medium heat for 1 minute, then add the lentils and stock and cook, stirring regularly, over low heat for 30–40 minutes, or until the liquid has evaporated and the lentils are tender.

Add the lentils to the eggplant and stir in the parsley and vinegar. Season well, drizzle with the extra virgin olive oil and serve.

Serves 4

## red potato salad with dill and mustard dressing

6 waxy, red-skinned potatoes,
   such as desiree (about
   1.1 kg/2 lb 8 oz)

**dill and mustard dressing**
1 tbs seeded mustard
1½ tbs chopped dill
2 tsp soft brown sugar
3 tbs red wine vinegar
4 tbs olive oil

Bring a large pot of lightly salted water to the boil. Add the potatoes and cook for 20 minutes, or until tender. Drain well and leave to cool slightly.

Meanwhile, make the dill and mustard dressing. Mix the mustard, dill, sugar and vinegar together in a jug, then whisk in the oil until well combined.

When the potatoes are cool enough to handle, cut them into 3 cm (1¼ inch) chunks. Gently toss the dressing through the warm potatoes, season to taste, and serve warm.

Serves 4

On an icy winter's evening, stoke the home fires, open a bottle of your favourite red and tuck into a bowl of this fulsome dish.

## warm roasted potato with spicy sausage

800 g (1 lb 12 oz) small waxy potatoes, unpeeled
2 tbs olive oil
1 tsp sea salt
4 small chorizo sausages (about 470 g/1 lb 1 oz), cut into
     1 cm (1/2 inch) slices
100 g (31/2 oz/1 small bunch) rocket (arugula), leaves
     trimmed and roughly torn
100 g (31/2 oz) semi-dried (sun-blushed) tomatoes
crusty bread, to serve

seeded mustard dressing
3 tbs olive oil
1 tbs seeded mustard
2 tbs sherry vinegar or white wine vinegar

Preheat the oven to 200°C (400°F/Gas 6). Scrub the potatoes and pat them dry. Put them in a roasting tin without any oil or seasoning and bake for 20 minutes, or until starting to soften. Remove from the oven and gently squash each potato using a potato masher, until the skins burst and they are slightly flattened. Lightly drizzle the oil over each potato, sprinkle with the sea salt and gently toss to coat. Roast for a further 10–15 minutes, or until crispy and golden.

Meanwhile, put a frying pan over high heat. Add the chorizo and dry-fry for about 5 minutes, or until cooked through and golden. Transfer to a serving dish with the rocket and tomatoes.

Put all the seeded mustard dressing ingredients in a small bowl. Whisk well and season lightly with salt and freshly ground black pepper.

Add the crispy potatoes to the salad, pour the dressing over and toss well. Serve hot or warm, with crusty bread.

Serves 4

warm roasted potato with spicy sausage

## warm prawn, rocket and feta salad

3 spring onions (scallions)
3 Roma (plum) tomatoes
1 small red capsicum
    (pepper)
400 g (14 oz) tin chickpeas,
    rinsed and drained
1/2 tbs chopped dill
2 tbs finely shredded basil
2 tbs olive oil
40 g (1 1/2 oz) butter

750 g (1 lb 10 oz) raw prawns
    (shrimp), peeled and
    deveined, tails intact
1 small red chilli, finely chopped
3 garlic cloves, crushed
1 1/2 tbs lemon juice
200 g (7 oz/2 small bunches)
    rocket (arugula), trimmed
100 g (3 1/2 oz) feta cheese,
    crumbled

Chop the spring onion, tomato and capsicum and place in a bowl with the chickpeas, dill and basil. Toss well.

Heat the oil and butter in a large frying pan. Add the prawns and cook, stirring, over high heat for 2 minutes. Add the chilli and garlic and continue cooking until the prawns turn pink. Remove from the heat and stir in the lemon juice.

Arrange the rocket on a large platter and top with the tomato mixture, then the prawn mixture. Scatter with the crumbled feta and serve.

Serves 4

## mini meatballs with couscous and yoghurt

600 g (1 lb 5 oz) lean minced
    (ground) beef
1 tsp chilli flakes
1 tsp ground cumin
2 tbs chopped pitted black olives
1 small onion, grated
2 tbs tomato paste (purée)
3–4 tbs olive oil

310 g (11 oz) instant couscous
250 g (9 oz/1 punnet) cherry
    tomatoes, halved
100 g (3¹/2 oz) roasted red
    capsicum (pepper), diced
200 g (7 oz) thick plain yoghurt
2 tbs lemon juice
2 tbs chopped parsley

Put the beef, chilli flakes, cumin, olives, onion and tomato paste in a bowl. Season, mix well with your hands and roll into 40 balls. Chill for 30 minutes.

Put 275 ml (9¹/2 fl oz) water in a saucepan with 2 tablespoons of the oil and 2 teaspoons of salt. Bring to the boil, remove from the heat and add the couscous. Stir, then cover and leave to stand for 2–3 minutes. Fluff up with a fork and add the tomatoes and capsicum. Season and mix well.

Heat the remaining oil in a large frying pan. Fry the meatballs over medium heat for 10–12 minutes, or until cooked through, then arrange them over the couscous. Mix the yoghurt, lemon juice and parsley together with 1 tablespoon water, drizzle over the meatballs and serve.

Serves 4

The sweet chilli marinade tenderizes the octopus, gently coaxing it into yielding a wealth of soft, spicy secrets.

## thai marinated octopus salad

8 baby octopus, or 4 large
    octopus cut in half
    (about 380 g/13 oz total)
250 ml (9 fl oz/1 cup) sweet
    chilli sauce
2 tbs lime juice

1 stem lemon grass, white part
    only, finely chopped
2 Lebanese (short) cucumbers
4 butter lettuce leaves, torn
4 large handfuls coriander
    (cilantro), with stalks

Using a small, sharp knife, carefully cut between the head and tentacles of the octopus, just below the eyes. Grasp the body of the octopus and push the beak out and up through the centre of the tentacles with your finger. Cut the eyes from the head of the octopus by slicing off a small disc and discard the eye section. To clean the octopus head, carefully slit through one side, avoiding the ink sac, and scrape out any gut from inside. Rinse under running water to remove any remaining gut.

Put the octopus in a non-metallic bowl and add the sweet chilli sauce, lime juice and lemon grass. Stir until well mixed and thoroughly coated. Cover with plastic wrap and leave to marinate for 4 hours.

Cut the cucumbers into 6 cm (2$^1$/$_2$ inch) lengths, scoop out the seeds and then slice the flesh into batons. Arrange the lettuce and coriander around the edge of a large serving plate.

Heat a frying pan or chargrill pan (griddle) to high. Remove the octopus from the marinade, reserving the marinade, and then fry them for about 3–4 minutes, or until tender and cooked through. Remove and pile in the middle of the serving plate.

Add the reserved marinade to the pan and heat through for 2 minutes. Stir the cucumber into the marinade to warm through, then spoon the marinade all over the salad and serve at once.

Serves 4

mini meatballs with couscous and yoghurt

## pumpkin and prawn salad with rocket

800 g (1 lb 10 oz) pumpkin,
    peeled and cut into
    3 cm (1 1/4 inch) cubes
2 small red onions, cut
    into thick wedges
1 tbs oil
2 cloves garlic, crushed

500 g (10 1/2 oz) cooked
    prawns (shrimp), peeled
    and deveined
200 g (7 oz) baby rocket
    (arugula) leaves
1–2 tbs balsamic vinegar
1 tbs olive oil

Preheat the oven to 200°C (400°F/Gas 6). Toss the pumpkin and onion in a large bowl with the oil and garlic. Spread in a single layer on a baking tray and bake for 25–30 minutes, or until tender. Transfer to a serving bowl, add the prawns and rocket and gently toss together.

Whisk together the vinegar and oil, and season to taste with sea salt and freshly ground black pepper. Drizzle over the salad and serve.

Serves 4

# mussel salad with warm saffron dressing

500 g (1 lb 2 oz) new potatoes
1 kg (2 lb 4 oz) black mussels
170 ml (5$^1$/$_2$ fl oz/$^2$/$_3$ cup) dry
  white wine
1 small onion, sliced

2 thyme sprigs
2 fresh or dried bay leaves
large pinch of powdered saffron
4 tbs sour cream
2 tsp chopped parsley

Cook the potatoes in salted boiling water until tender. Drain and leave to cool slightly. Meanwhile, scrub the mussels with a stiff brush and pull out the hairy beards. Discard any broken mussels, or open ones that don't close when tapped on the bench. Rinse well under running water.

Put the wine, onion, thyme, bay leaves and half the mussels in a pot. Cover and cook over high heat, stirring once, for 3–4 minutes, or until the mussels start to open. Remove the mussels as they open and discard any unopened ones. Cook the remaining mussels and leave to cool slightly. Strain the mussel stock, reserving 125 ml (4 fl oz/$^1$/$_2$ cup). While the liquid is still warm, stir in the saffron. Whisk in the sour cream and season well.

Quarter any large potatoes and halve the small ones. Remove the mussels from their shells, place in a serving bowl with the potatoes and gently mix the warm saffron dressing through. Sprinkle with the parsley and serve.

Serves 4

Lovely lamb gets an extra lift from the herbal scent of fresh mint and a burst of tiny sweet tomatoes.

## minted lamb salad with haloumi

2 tbs olive oil
500 g (1 lb 2 oz) lamb fillets,
    trimmed
1 red coral lettuce, leaves torn
8 yellow teardrop tomatoes
8 cherry tomatoes
100 g (3 1/2 oz) haloumi cheese,
    cut into 1 cm x 4 cm
    (1/2 x 1 1/2 inch) fingers

mint and mustard dressing
3 tbs olive oil
1 tbs white wine vinegar
1/2 tsp French mustard
1 tbs chopped mint
1/2 tsp sugar

Heat half the oil in a heavy-based pan over medium–high heat. Add the lamb fillets and cook, turning frequently, for 7–8 minutes for a medium-rare result — do not overcook the lamb, it should still be pink in the middle. Transfer to a plate, cover loosely with foil and allow to rest for 5–10 minutes. Thinly slice the fillets on the diagonal.

Divide the lettuce between four serving plates and arrange the tomatoes and lamb slices over the top.

Put all the mint and mustard dressing ingredients in a small screw-top jar, then shake well and set aside.

Heat the remaining oil in the pan. Add the haloumi and cook over medium heat for 2 minutes or until golden, turning occasionally. Drain on cumpled paper towels and arrange on top of the salad. Briefly shake the dressing again, drizzle over the salad and serve immediately.

Serves 4

pumpkin and prawn salad with rocket

## mushroom and shredded chicken salad

1–2 tbs olive oil
200 g (7 oz) small button
    mushrooms
200 g (7 oz) other mixed
    mushrooms (such as Swiss
    brown and shiitake), larger
    ones halved or quartered
400 g (14 oz) cooked chicken,
    shredded
200 g (7 oz) mixed salad leaves

**lime and soy dressing**

2 tbs lime juice
1 tbs soy sauce
2 tbs olive oil
1 tbs sweet chilli sauce
1 tbs red wine vinegar

Heat 1 tablespoon of the oil in a frying pan. Add the mushrooms and cook over medium heat for 2–3 minutes, or until softened. Toss in a large bowl with the shredded chicken.

Combine all the lime and soy dressing ingredients in a small bowl or jug, mix well and pour two-thirds over the warm mushrooms.

Arrange the salad leaves in a serving dish and toss through the remaining dressing. Top with the chicken and mushrooms and serve warm.

Serves 4

## warm chicken and pasta salad

375 g (13 oz) penne
125 ml (4 fl oz/$1/2$ cup) olive oil
4 slender eggplants (aubergines), thinly sliced on the diagonal
2 chicken breast fillets
2 tsp lemon juice
2 handfuls parsley, chopped
270 g (9$3/4$ oz) chargrilled red capsicum (pepper) slices
175 g (7 oz/1 bunch) asparagus spears, trimmed and blanched
85 g (3 oz) semi-dried (sun-blushed) tomatoes, sliced
grated Parmesan cheese, to serve

Cook the pasta in a large pot of rapidly boiling salted water until al dente. Drain, return to the pan and keep warm.

Meanwhile, heat 2 tablespoons of the oil in a large frying pan. Fry the eggplant over high heat for 4–5 minutes, or until golden and cooked through; remove. Heat another 2 tablespoons of oil in the pan, reduce the heat to medium and cook the chicken for 4–5 minutes on each side, or until lightly browned and cooked through. Allow to cool, then thickly slice.

Put the remaining oil in a small screw-top jar with the lemon juice and parsley and shake well. Return the pasta to the heat and toss through the dressing, chicken, eggplant, capsicum, asparagus and tomato to warm through. Season with black pepper, scatter with Parmesan and serve.

Serves 4

The mellow warmth of roast garlic and the sharp tang of feta balance the sweetness of the beetroot and sweet potato.

### roasted beetroot and sweet potato salad with feta

350 g (12 oz) baby beetroot, trimmed and scrubbed
350 g (12 oz) orange sweet potato, peeled and cut into 2 cm (3/4 inch) chunks
3 tbs garlic oil (see Note)
1 garlic bulb
20 g (3/4 oz) butter
3 tbs olive oil

1 red onion, cut into wedges
1 tbs balsamic vinegar
1 tsp soft brown sugar
150 g (5 1/2 oz) baby English spinach leaves
2 rosemary sprigs
2 tbs lemon juice
1 tbs shredded basil
120 g (4 1/2 oz) feta cheese

Preheat the oven to 180°C (350°F/Gas 4). Arrange the beetroot on a baking tray. Brush the sweet potato with the garlic oil and season; place on another baking tray with the whole garlic bulb. Roast the vegetables for 35–40 minutes, or until tender when pierced with a knife. Remove from the oven and allow to cool, then peel the beetroot, wearing gloves.

Heat the butter and 1 tablespoon of the olive oil in a small saucepan. When the butter has melted, add the onion and cook over medium heat, stirring occasionally, for 15 minutes, or until soft. Add the vinegar and sugar and cook for 3–5 minutes, or until the onion is golden and starting to caramelize. Place in a serving bowl with the roasted beetroot, sweet potato, spinach and rosemary leaves and mix together gently.

Slip the roasted garlic cloves from their skins into a small bowl. Add the remaining olive oil, lemon juice and basil and whisk together well to make a dressing, then season to taste. Crumble the feta over the salad, drizzle with the roasted garlic dressing and serve.

Note: If you are unable to obtain garlic oil, you can make your own by steeping some crushed garlic in extra virgin olive oil for 2 hours, then straining it. Alternatively, use plain olive oil for this recipe.

Serves 4

mushroom and shredded chicken salad

## squid and scallops with chermoula dressing

8 baby squid, cleaned and rinsed
200 g (7 oz) scallops, without roe
2 tbs oil
150 g (5¹/₂ oz/1 bunch) rocket
    (arugula), trimmed
3 ripe Roma (plum) tomatoes,
    chopped
2 oranges, peeled and
    segmented

chermoula dressing
4 large handfuls coriander
    (cilantro), finely chopped
2¹/₂ large handfuls flat-leaf
    (Italian) parsley, chopped
2 tsp ground cumin
1 tsp ground paprika
3 tbs lime juice
3 tbs olive oil

394

Put the squid in a bowl of water with ¹/₄ teaspoon salt. Mix well, then chill for 30 minutes. Drain well, then cut the tubes into long thin strips and the tentacles into pieces. Rinse the scallops and pat them dry with paper towels.

Heat the oil in a large deep frying pan. Cook the squid in batches over high heat for 1 minute, or until they turn white. Remove and drain. Fry the scallops in small batches over high heat for 1 minute on each side, until golden.

Arrange the rocket on a large platter, then top with the seafood, tomato and orange segments. Quickly whisk the chermoula dressing ingredients together in a non-metallic bowl, pour over the seafood and serve.

Serves 4

## warm pasta and crab salad

300 g (10$1/2$ oz) thin spaghetti
2 tbs olive oil
20 g ($3/4$ oz) butter, chopped
350 g (12 oz) fresh crab meat
1 red capsicum (pepper), cut
   into thin strips

1$1/2$ tsp finely grated lemon zest
3 tbs grated Parmesan cheese
2 tbs snipped chives
3 tbs chopped parsley

Break all the spaghetti in half and cook in a large pot of rapidly boiling salted water until al dente. Drain well, then place in a large serving bowl and toss with the oil and butter.

Add the crab meat, capsicum, lemon zest, Parmesan, chives and parsley, and toss to combine. Sprinkle with freshly ground black pepper and serve.

Serves 4

## italian-style chicken and pasta salad

400 g (14 oz) chicken breast
    fillets
3 tbs lemon juice
2 small garlic cloves, crushed
1 tbs seasoned lemon pepper
1 1/2 tbs olive oil
300 g (10 1/2 oz) penne, cooked
100 g (3 1/2 oz) prosciutto,
    sliced into thin strips
1 Lebanese (short) cucumber,
    cut in half lengthways,
    then sliced
50 g (1 3/4 oz/1/3 cup) thinly
    sliced sun-dried tomatoes

45 g (1 1/2 oz/1/3 cup) pitted
    black olives, halved
4 bottled artichoke hearts,
    halved
25 g (1 oz/1/4 cup) shaved
    Parmesan cheese

creamy basil sauce
3 tbs olive oil
1 tbs white wine vinegar
1 tsp Dijon mustard
3 tsp cornflour (cornstarch)
170 ml (5 1/2 oz/2/3 cup) cream
4 tbs shredded basil

Flatten the chicken breasts slightly with a mallet or rolling pin. Mix the lemon juice and garlic in a bowl, add the chicken fillets and turn until coated all over. Cover with plastic wrap and refrigerate for at least 3 hours or overnight, turning occasionally.

Drain the chicken and coat in the seasoned lemon pepper. Heat the oil in a large heavy-based frying pan. Add the chicken and cook over medium heat for 4–5 minutes on each side, or until lightly browned and cooked through. Remove from the heat, allow to cool, then cut into thin slices.

To make the creamy basil sauce, combine the oil, vinegar and mustard in a saucepan with a little salt and freshly ground pepper. Blend the cornflour with 4 tablespoons of water in a small bowl or jug until smooth. Add to the pan and whisk over medium heat for 2 minutes, or until the sauce boils and thickens. Add the cream and basil, check for salt, and stir until heated through.

Combine the pasta, chicken, prosciutto, cucumber, tomato, olives and artichoke in a large serving bowl. Pour over the warm sauce and toss gently to combine. Scatter with the shaved Parmesan and serve.

Serves 4

warm pasta and crab salad

## eggplant salad

10 slender eggplants (aubergines)
2 tbs peanut oil
3 red Asian shallots, finely sliced
2 garlic cloves, crushed
1 red chilli, finely chopped
1 boiled egg, peeled and diced
1 tbs fried red Asian shallot flakes
2 tbs coriander (cilantro) leaves

dressing
1 tsp grated palm sugar or
    soft brown sugar
2 tbs soy sauce
1–2 tsp fish sauce
2 tbs lime juice
1 tbs toasted sesame seeds

Preheat the oven to 200°C (400°F/Gas 6). Put the eggplant in a roasting tin with half the oil and toss to coat. Bake for 15 minutes, or until tender. Remove from the oven and leave to cool, then peel away the skin and cut the flesh into 2 cm (3/4 inch) chunks.

Heat the remaining oil in a frying pan. Add the shallot, garlic and chilli and cook over medium heat for 2 minutes, or until soft. Transfer to a mortar and pestle and pound into a paste, then mix with the eggplant.

Put the dressing ingredients in a bowl and stir until the sugar has dissolved. Spoon the eggplant mixture onto a serving platter and top with the egg, shallot flakes and coriander. Pour the dressing over and serve at once.

Serves 4

## roasted fennel, beetroot and smoked trout salad

12 baby beetroot
2–3 tbs olive oil
2 large fennel bulbs (about
    650 g/1 lb 7 oz each)
100 g (3 1/2 oz) smoked trout
    fillet, broken into chunks
crusty bread, to serve

**horseradish dressing**
175 g (6 oz/2/3 cup) sour cream
1 tbs creamed horseradish
1 tbs lemon juice
2 tbs snipped chives

Preheat the oven to 200°C (400°F/Gas 6). Wearing gloves, peel the beetroot, then cut the bulbs into chunks. Place in a large roasting tin and drizzle with 2 tablespoons of the oil. Season with salt and pepper and toss to coat, then cover with foil and roast for 40–45 minutes, or until tender.

Meanwhile, cut off and discard the stalks and fronds from the fennel. Cut the bulbs into quarters and blanch in boiling salted water for 5 minutes, or until tender. Drain well and cut into smaller wedges. Add to the beetroot for the final 30 minutes of cooking, adding a little extra oil if needed.

Put the beetroot and fennel in a serving dish with the smoked trout. Combine the horseradish dressing ingredients in a small bowl and dollop over the salad. Serve warm with crusty bread.

Serves 4

Roasting tomatoes intensifies their sweetness and reveals a depth of flavour that exquisitely complements the seared lamb.

## lamb with roasted tomatoes

6 vine-ripened tomatoes
4 garlic cloves, finely chopped
1 tbs chopped oregano
1 tbs chopped parsley
3 tbs olive oil
525 g (1 lb 3 oz/3 bunches)
    asparagus spears, trimmed
2 lamb backstraps or loin fillets
    (about 500 g/1 lb 2 oz)

mint yoghurt dressing
1 tbs red wine vinegar
$^1/_2$ Lebanese (short) cucumber,
    finely diced
100 g (3$^1/_2$ oz) thick plain
    yoghurt
2 tsp chopped mint
$^1/_2$ tsp ground cumin
1 tbs olive oil

Preheat the oven to 180°C (350°F/Gas 4). Cut the tomatoes in half and scoop out the seeds. In a small bowl, mix together the garlic, oregano and parsley, then sprinkle the mixture into the tomato shells. Put the tomatoes on a rack in a roasting tin, then drizzle with 1 tablespoon of the oil and roast for 1 hour. Remove the tomatoes from the oven, cut them into halves and keep warm.

Put the asparagus in the roasting tin and drizzle with another tablespoon of the oil. Season and roast for 10 minutes.

Meanwhile, heat the remaining oil in a frying pan. Season the lamb well and cook over medium–high heat for 5 minutes on each side, then remove from the heat, cover with foil and set aside for 5–10 minutes to rest.

Put all the mint yoghurt dressing ingredients in a small jug and whisk together well. Arrange the asparagus on a serving platter and top with the roasted tomatoes. Slice the lamb on the diagonal and arrange on top of the tomatoes. Drizzle with the dressing and serve immediately.

Serves 4

roasted fennel, beetroot and smoked trout salad

## minced pork and noodle salad

1 tbs peanut oil
500 g (1 lb 2 oz) minced
   (ground) pork
2 garlic cloves, finely chopped
1 stem lemon grass, white
   part only, finely chopped
3 red Asian shallots, finely sliced
3 tsp finely grated fresh ginger
1 small red chilli, finely chopped
5 makrut (kaffir lime) leaves,
   very finely shredded
170 g (6 oz) glass (mung bean)
   noodles

60 g (2¼ oz) baby English
   spinach leaves
4 large handfuls coriander
   (cilantro), chopped
1 large handful mint leaves

### dressing
1½ tbs grated palm sugar
   or soft brown sugar
2 tbs fish sauce
4 tbs lime juice
2 tsp sesame oil
2 tsp peanut oil

Heat a wok until very hot, add the oil and swirl to coat. Stir-fry the pork in batches over high heat for 5 minutes, or until golden. Add the garlic, lemon grass, shallot, ginger, chilli and lime leaves and stir-fry until fragrant.

Cover the noodles with boiling water to soften. Rinse, drain and toss in a bowl with the pork, spinach, coriander and mint. Whisk together the dressing ingredients and toss through the salad. Season with pepper and serve.

Serves 4

# roasted vegetables with pan-fried garlic breadcrumbs

3 zucchini (courgettes), sliced
225 g (8 oz) button mushrooms,
   larger ones halved
1 red onion, cut into 8 wedges
1 red capsicum (pepper), diced
3 tbs olive oil
1 garlic clove, crushed

40 g (1$^1$/2 oz/$^1$/2 cup) breadcrumbs,
   made from day-old bread

dressing
1 tbs olive oil
2 tbs ready-made pesto
1 tbs lemon juice

Preheat the oven to 200°C (400°F/Gas 6). Put all the vegetables in a large baking dish. Drizzle over 2 tablespoons of the oil, add a little salt and pepper and shake the pan to coat all the vegetables in the oil. Roast for 30 minutes, or until all the vegetables are tender.

Combine the dressing ingredients in a large serving bowl. Add the roasted vegetables, toss gently and leave for 10 minutes for the flavours to absorb.

Heat the remaining oil in a frying pan and fry the garlic over medium heat for about 30 seconds. Increase the heat, add the breadcrumbs and fry for 2–3 minutes, or until golden, shaking the pan and stirring the crumbs. Toss the toasted breadcrumbs through the salad and serve.

Serves 4

Seriously spicy and fabulously fragrant, this tortilla-topped salad offers a healthy taste of Mexico without the heft.

### blackened chicken with crispy tortillas

4 vine-ripened tomatoes, cut into 1 cm (1/2 inch) slices
1 tsp caster (superfine) sugar
1 red onion, sliced
150 ml (5 fl oz) olive oil
1 tsp ground oregano
2 1/2 tsp ground cumin
1 1/4 tsp garlic salt
1/2 tsp cayenne pepper
4 small chicken breast fillets (about 600 g/1 lb 5 oz)

2 corn tortillas, each 16 cm (6 1/4 inches) round, cut into 2 cm (3/4 inch) strips
2 handfuls coriander (cilantro) leaves

guacamole dressing
1 ripe avocado
60 g (2 oz/1/4 cup) sour cream
100 ml (3 1/2 fl oz) milk
2 tbs lime juice

Arrange the tomato slices in a wide dish, sprinkle with the sugar and season well. Layer the onion over the top and drizzle with 3 tablespoons of the oil. Cover and refrigerate for 20 minutes.

To make the guacomole dressing, blend the avocado, sour cream, milk and lime juice in a food processor with 4 tablespoons of water for about 1 minute, or until smooth. Season.

Combine the oregano, cumin, garlic salt and cayenne pepper in a small bowl and use it to coat the chicken breasts, pressing down firmly with your fingers. Heat 1$^1$/2 tablespoons of oil over medium heat in a large non-stick frying pan until hot. Cook the chicken breasts for 4–5 minutes on each side, or until cooked through. Remove and leave to cool a little.

In the same pan, heat the remaining oil. Fry the tortilla strips until golden, turning once during cooking.

Arrange the tomato and onion slices in a circle on four serving plates. Slice each chicken breast on the diagonal into 2 cm ($^3$/4 inch) strips and place on top of the tomato. Spoon the dressing over and top with the tortilla strips. Scatter with the coriander and serve hot.

Serves 4

roasted vegetables with pan-fried garlic breadcrumbs

## warm mixed bean salad

2 tbs olive oil
125 ml (4 fl oz/$^1/_2$ cup) tomato
   juice
2 tbs chopped flat-leaf (Italian)
   parsley
pinch of sugar
3 garlic cloves

400 g (14 oz) tin borlotti beans,
   drained and rinsed
400 g (14 oz) tin cannellini
   beans, drained and rinsed
2 tomatoes, diced
4 thick slices crusty bread

Put 1 tablespoon of the oil in a small bowl with the tomato juice, parsley and sugar. Crush two of the garlic cloves and stir them into the mixture.

Put the borlotti and cannellini beans in a frying pan, add the tomato mixture and place over medium heat for about 5 minutes, or until well warmed through. Toss through the diced tomato and season to taste.

Meanwhile, toast the bread slices. Cut the remaining garlic clove and rub the cut side all over the bread. Drizzle with the remaining oil and serve hot with the warm beans.

Serves 4

## warm lentil and rice salad

185 ml (6 fl oz/3/4 cup) olive oil
30 g (1 oz) butter
3 large red onions, finely sliced
3 garlic cloves, crushed
2 tsp ground cinnamon
2 tsp ground sweet paprika
2 tsp ground cumin

2 tsp ground coriander
140 g (5 oz/3/4 cup) green lentils
150 g (5 1/2 oz/3/4 cup) basmati
    rice
3 spring onions (scallions),
    finely chopped

Heat the oil and butter in a frying pan. When the butter has melted, add the onion and garlic and cook over low heat, stirring, for 30 minutes, or until very soft. Stir in the cinnamon, paprika, cumin and ground coriander and cook for a few minutes longer, or until aromatic. Keep warm.

Meanwhile, bring a pot of water to the boil, add the rice and cook until the grains are just tender. While the rice is cooking, bring another pot of water to the boil, add the lentils and cook until just tender.

Drain the rice and lentils well, then transfer to a large serving bowl and mix through the onion mixture, spring onion and freshly ground black pepper to taste. Serve warm.

Serves 4

Pancetta, sage and parsley bring a continental chutzpah to this sophisticated salad, with a splash of sherry to help make merry.

## fusilli salad with sherry vinaigrette

200 g (7 oz) fusilli or other spiral pasta
160 g (5³/4 oz/1¹/3 cups) small cauliflower florets
80 g (2³/4 oz/¹/2 cup) toasted pine nuts
4 tbs olive oil
10 slices pancetta
1 small handful small sage leaves
1¹/2 tbs finely chopped red Asian shallots
1 tbs sherry vinegar
1 small red chilli, finely chopped
2 garlic cloves, crushed
1 tsp soft brown sugar
2 tbs orange juice
1 large handful parsley, finely chopped
25 g (1 oz/¹/4 cup) shaved Parmesan cheese

Cook the pasta in a large pot of rapidly boiling salted water until al dente. Drain, rinse under cold water and drain again.

Blanch the cauliflower florets in boiling water for 2–3 minutes, then drain and cool. Place in a large serving bowl with the pasta and pine nuts.

Heat 1 tablespoon of the oil in a non-stick frying pan and cook the pancetta for 2 minutes, or until crisp. Remove and drain on crumpled paper towels. Add 1 more tablespoon of oil and fry the sage leaves for 1 minute, or until crisp. Remove and drain on crumpled paper towels.

Heat the remaining oil in the pan, add the shallots and cook gently for 2 minutes, or until soft. Remove from the heat, then stir in the vinegar, chilli, garlic, sugar, orange juice and parsley. Pour the warm dressing over the pasta and toss gently. Crumble the pancetta over the top and scatter with the sage leaves and shaved Parmesan. Serve warm.

Serves 4

warm mixed bean salad

# warm thai tuna salad

650 g (1 lb 7 oz) fresh tuna steaks
1 tbs olive oil
2 tbs oyster sauce
2 tbs soy sauce
2 tbs lime juice
300 g (10½ oz) dried egg noodles
125 g (4½ oz) baby corn, halved
150 g (5½ oz) snowpeas
    (mangetout), tailed

coriander chilli dressing
2 tbs fish sauce
2 tbs lime juice
2 tbs Thai sweet chilli sauce
2 tbs vegetable oil
1 small red chilli, chopped
3 tbs chopped coriander
    (cilantro)

Put the tuna in a shallow dish in a single layer. Whisk together the oil, oyster sauce, soy sauce and lime juice and pour the mixture over the tuna, turning to coat all over. Cover and refrigerate for 30 minutes.

Cook the noodles according to the packet instructions, adding the corn and snowpeas for the final 45 seconds. Drain well, then toss in a serving bowl. Combine the dressing ingredients and mix half through the noodles.

Heat a chargrill pan (griddle) to high. Cook the tuna for 3–4 minutes on each side, so it's still pink in the middle. Cool slightly, then slice into strips. Serve separately or over the noodles, with the remaining dressing on the side.

Serves 4

## salmon and green bean salad

2 tsp olive oil
275 g (9³/4 oz) salmon fillet,
    skin removed
vegetable oil, for deep-frying
3 garlic cloves, thinly sliced
150 g (5¹/2 oz) white sweet
    potato, thinly sliced
75 g (2¹/2 oz) green beans,
    trimmed and blanched
1 small red onion, thinly sliced

1 tbs toasted sesame seeds
1 mizuna lettuce, leaves torn

### lime and tahini dressing

2 garlic cloves, crushed
1¹/2 tbs tahini
3 tsp rice vinegar
1¹/2 tbs lime juice
3 tsp soy sauce
2 tbs olive oil

Heat the oil in a frying pan. Cook the salmon over medium heat for 2–3 minutes on each side. Cool slightly, then cut into chunks.

Fill a deep-fryer or wok one-third full of oil and heat to 180°C (350°F), or until a cube of bread dropped in the oil browns in 15 seconds. In separate batches, cook the garlic and sweet potato until golden and crisp, then drain.

Whisk together the dressing ingredients. Toss the garlic and sweet potato in a bowl with the beans, onion, sesame seeds and lettuce. Divide between four serving plates, top with salmon, drizzle with the dressing and serve.

Serves 4

Baby English spinach makes a delicate bed for the chicken,

with its refreshing dressing of garlic, mint and cider vinegar.

## warm minted chicken and pasta salad

250 g (9 oz) cotelli or other spiral pasta
125 ml (4 fl oz/1/2 cup) olive oil
1 large red capsicum (pepper)
3 chicken breast fillets
6 spring onions (scallions), cut into 2 cm (3/4 inch) lengths
4 garlic cloves, thinly sliced
4 tbs cider vinegar
3 large handfuls mint leaves, chopped
100 g (31/2 oz) baby English spinach leaves

Cook the pasta in a large pot of rapidly boiling salted water until al dente. Drain, transfer to a large serving bowl and stir in 1 tablespoon of the oil.

Meanwhile, cut the capsicum into large flat pieces and remove the seeds and membranes. Cook, skin-side-up, under a hot grill (broiler) for

8–10 minutes, or until the skin blackens and blisters. Leave to cool in a plastic bag, then peel away the skin and cut the capsicum into thin strips.

Place the chicken between two sheets of plastic wrap and press with the palm of your hand until slightly flattened.

Heat 1 tablespoon of the oil in a large frying pan. Add the chicken and cook over medium heat for 4–5 minutes on each side, or until lightly browned and cooked through. Remove from the pan and allow to cool a little. Cut into thin slices and add to the pasta.

Heat another tablespoon of the oil in the pan. Add the spring onion, garlic and roasted capsicum and cook, stirring, for 2–3 minutes, or until starting to soften. Add the remaining oil, vinegar and most of the mint leaves and stir until warmed through. Add to the pasta with the spinach and remaining mint, toss well and season to taste. Serve warm.

Serves 4

warm thai tuna salad

# warm choy sum salad

1 bunch choy sum (about
   370 g/13 oz)
2 tbs peanut oil
3 tsp finely grated fresh ginger
2 garlic cloves, finely chopped
2 tsp sugar

2 tsp sesame oil
2 tbs soy sauce
1 tbs lemon juice
2 tsp toasted sesame seeds

Trim the ends from the choy sum and slice the leaves in half. Steam for about 2 minutes, or until just wilted.

Heat a small saucepan to very hot, add the peanut oil and swirl to coat the pan. Add the ginger and garlic and stir-fry for 1 minute. Add the sugar, sesame oil, soy sauce and lemon juice and heat until hot.

Arrange the choy sum on a serving plate and pour over the hot dressing. Season to taste, scatter with the sesame seeds and serve.

Serves 4

## warm pork salad with blue cheese croutons

125 ml (4 fl oz/1/2 cup) olive oil
1 large garlic clove, crushed
400 g (14 oz) pork fillet, cut
    into 5 mm (1/4 inch) slices
1 small or 1/2 a large baguette

100 g (31/2 oz) blue cheese,
    crumbled
2 tbs sherry vinegar
1/2 tsp soft brown sugar
150 g (51/2 oz) mixed salad leaves

Put the oil and garlic in a screw-top jar and shake well. Heat 2 teaspoons of the garlic oil mixture in a frying pan over medium–high heat. Add half the pork slices and cook for 1 minute on each side, then remove and keep warm. Add another 2 teaspoons of the garlic oil and cook the remaining pork. Remove, keep warm and season all the pork with salt and pepper.

Cut the bread into 20 thin slices and spread on a baking tray. Brush the tops with a little garlic oil and cook under a hot griller (broiler) until golden, about 1–2 minutes. Turn the bread over, sprinkle with the blue cheese, then grill for about 30 seconds to melt the cheese.

Add the vinegar and sugar to the remaining garlic oil and shake well. Put the salad leaves in a large bowl, add the pork and pour on the salad dressing. Toss well. Place a mound of salad in the middle of four serving plates and arrange five croutons around the edge of each. Serve at once.

Serves 4

# index

427

428